Storymaker

Storymaker

The Art of Creating and Sharing Stories with Children

GILES
ABBOTT

For Sooz,
With undying love and thanks for the way you showed the way, lit the way and lead the way. Nothing without you Belle!
G ;{~

First published 2025

The History Press
97 St George's Place, Cheltenham,
Gloucestershire, GL50 3QB
www.thehistorypress.co.uk

British Library Cataloguing in Publication Data.
A catalogue record for this book is available from the British Library.

ISBN 978 1 80399 918 0

Typesetting and origination by The History Press.
Printed and bound in Great Britain by TJ Books, Padstow, Cornwall.

The History Press proudly supports
Trees for Life
www.treesforlife.org.uk

EU Authorised Representative: Easy Access System Europe
Mustamäe tee 50, 10621 Tallinn, Estonia
gpst.request@easproject.com

Contents

Introduction

What is This Book?

It's bedtime. Your child or grandchild is snugly tucked up in their bed, their head, cradled in soft pillows, is turned towards you. Their eyes meet yours and there is an understanding in that look, an anticipation. So you open the book and begin, softly, to read. Soon, your child's eyes are seeing not the room, not you, but the story you are sharing. You love this sharing.

But what do you do on a long car journey? You can't read a book when you're driving! What about when waiting in the interminable queue at the doctors or at hospital? Or when waiting to board a plane, a coach, a ferry? Perhaps your child is restless, perhaps distressed, what can you do? It's not like you can simply conjure a story out of thin air.

Actually, you can. It is in your nature, it is in your power, it is your very own, very special gift. You are a born storyteller and this book, using simple, tried and tested techniques, will help release the magnetic, spellbinding storyteller in you. You will learn how to create stories that, though they have never been told before, have been tested and proven over hundreds, perhaps thousands of years. You will learn simple, easy to remember structures, recipes, you might say, to guide your imagination so that you will never get lost, never lose your child's attention, never fail to reward their longing for a story. You will learn simple ways to help you remember these recipes, so you can call them to mind instantly, the right recipe for the right occasion, and you will open worlds of wonder in your child's mind.

Or perhaps you are a schoolteacher? It might be an away day, a school camp or just a long traffic jam and a coach full of kids. Imagine if you could confidently conjure up a story for them or, better still, conjure up a story *with* them, recruiting their active participation in the creative process? Or perhaps you work with older children - what if you had the power to create a story to tell your pupils that opens up discussion of key topics like citizenship, justice, equality, freedom, societal norms and biases? You can, and these techniques do not date as children grow older. As they grow, this book will help you to develop and deepen the stories you tell to them and with them, each one unique and special to you, to them, to that moment. As they mature, so too do the stories you tell them. All that time you are looking, not into a book, but straight into your child's eyes. They are not looking at a screen; they are looking at you and you are not showing them someone else's pictures in a book because they can see, vividly, their own pictures in their own minds, which they have created in response to your storytelling. In this telling, you are helping their minds and personalities to develop.

Now, you might say that you could never tell a story like this or that storyteller or actor you may have heard, and it's true, you can't. But you can do something better than that - you can tell a story like *you*, and that is what your child most wants. Whether you're a parent, a grandparent or a teacher or carer, you are the one who has that connection to that child or those children. And when they are older, you can teach these techniques to them, and just see what it does to their schoolwork! And when they are all grown up, with children of their own, and they say, 'Mum/Dad, d'you remember, when I was little, you used to just make up stories, but they were really good? How did you do that?' You won't have forgotten. In fact, you've been wondering when they'd ask. You can tell them the story of your storytelling. That story starts here, now.

☞ Who is Your Guide?

At this stage you might be wondering, who is this author and how are they qualified to guide me on this journey? Fair point - you should never start a journey without first checking the credentials of your guide. Furthermore, I am not, in this book, attempting a definitive, exhaustive, nor comprehensive academic study of story and storytelling. I shan't be quoting sources and authors and authorities. I can't. You'll find out why in a moment but I'm afraid the best I can do is lead you on a personal journey based on my personal knowledge and experience. Best I tell you who this person is, so allow me to introduce myself.

I was born and brought up in London, starting in the 1970s, and, after school, I did my BA in English Language and Literature at St Catherine's College, University of Oxford. Both my parents had been, before my birth, secondary school English teachers so that's the ocean I swam in as a child.

With one important difference. When I was very young my mother would collect me and my big brother from primary school, sit us down and then take down a battered copy of Homer. Instead of TV, we listened to her reading, episodically, first the entire *Iliad* and then the entire *Odyssey*. She has since told me it was a rotten translation, but it's the copy she had as a child and so she shared it with us. So, while we also watched TV, before we got TV, we got to meet Laughter-Loving Aphrodite, Flashing-Eyed Athena, Sky-Shaking Zeus and Achilles, Neoptolemus, both Ajaxes, Agamemnon and Clytemnestra, Menelaus and Helen and Paris, Hector, Priam, Cassandra, Penelope and, of course, Odysseus. I'm not looking these names up – they are part of me.

I thrilled at these riveting stories, learned to read myself and, as soon as I could read without stabilisers, I found books suitable for my age so, *The Greek Myths* by Roger Lancelyn Green and collections of Norse myths (called *Horned Helmet*, but I forget the author's name). When I was a little older I devoured collections of Greek and Norse and Celtic mythology, and authors like J.R.R. Tolkien, Alan Garner, Susan Cooper and many more. Naturally, my interests were guided towards the study of literature and that's what I did, hence my BA, but even when I was doing my BA in literature I retained a keen interest in the pre-literate.

Then, in 1998, when I had just turned 25, I very rapidly lost all the central, and therefore focal, vision in my right eye. It took five days. Then, five months later, I lost the central vision in my left eye. This took place during a coach journey from Leeds to London so, in total, about four hours. It took four hours to lose entirely my ability to read a book, a newspaper, a face.

I'm not turning this into a sob-story, a pity party. I have now been registered blind for most of my life[1] and it has been and continues to be a wonderful, exciting and joyful life. But it was very, very hard for at least seven years as I struggled to come to terms with my changed reality, my disability, its limitations and the loss of something I had dearly loved all my life – the joy of reading.

But in 1999, my girlfriend, who is now my wife, heard from a friend that, in the village 4 miles down the valley from where we were living,[2] a pub called the Stubbing Wharf was hosting an evening with a group of storytellers. I was astonished – did people still *do* that?

So we went to the Stubbing Wharf pub in Hebden Bridge. We found seats in a crowded room at the top of the pub and I listened, mesmerised and delighted as Alan Sparkes, Christine McMahon, Rachel Lowes and Paul Degnan, known collectively as the Shaggy Dog Storytellers, took turns to tell dazzling folk stories located in and around the Calder Valley. I was a child again, sat as if at my mother's table, my blinded eyes dancing with delight. I couldn't see what was in front of me, couldn't see what the storytellers looked like, but I *could* see, very clearly, what was not right in front of me at all, but there it was, clearly visible in that second sight, my imagination. It felt like coming home.

Throughout the evening, host and club founder Alan Sparkes told the audience that, after the featured storytellers had performed the first two forty-five-minute-long sets, and after suitable breaks to 'refresh your drinks and undergo nicotine replacement therapy', the last forty-five minutes would take the form of an open spot. If anyone in the audience had a story to tell, five to ten minutes long, then if they had a word with him, or with Christine, then they'd try to fit everyone in. He also kept advertising a beginners' course that he would be running in a few months' time in partnership with a professional storyteller from Manchester called Clive Hopwood, and there were still some spaces available ...

My mind was reeling. You could be a *professional* storyteller? Take something as magical and fun as this and make it your job? I knew that I would be unable to afford a place on the beginners' course because, due to my sight loss and other symptoms of the accompanying illness, I had lost my job.[3] My girlfriend Sooz had quit her job to look after me and so we two were living on statutory sick pay, which really doesn't go very far. But, I was thinking, there might be a book available about how to tell traditional stories and Sooz could read it to me, and then I might be able to craft and practise, maybe in about six months' time, a ten-minute story that *I* could tell in the open spot?

There was snag though. After my sight loss, Sooz had to read me my correspondence (bank, employer, that kind of thing – this is all before email) and I had identified something that was afterwards confirmed by specialists, namely that Sooz is acutely dyslexic/aphasic[4] and that, when she was reading to me, she saw all the words equally well at the same time but could not decide the order in which to say them and neither could she plot a simple horizontal journey from left to right through the text. Listening, I realised she was saying all the right words but not necessarily in the right order. That was the dyslexia. Further to that was the aphasia, which meant that she would often create spoonerisms, accurately swapping the initial letters of pairs or even three successive words and, sometimes, when reading or just speaking, she would say entire, sometimes multi-syllable words accurately but backwards. It would be exhausting for her to read a whole book to me, but I was nonetheless confident that she would. Typical bloke.

Actually, she did better. That night in the pub, after the break the host, Alan, asked us all to welcome to the floor a newcomer to the club, someone who had never told a story in public before, so would we all give a warm Shaggy Dog welcome to ... Sooz.

I nearly fell off my chair. My Sooz, the one who sometimes speaks entire words backwards, left her place next to me, walked to the front of the room and told a story. She told brilliantly. She engaged their attention, held their attention, rewarded their attention as she told, confidently, a story about her father's childhood in Jamaica. She received an enthusiastic round of applause when she finished and, by the time she'd sat down, I had realised that I didn't need her to read me a book. I didn't need to go on a beginners' course.

'Where did that come from?' I gasped.

'I did it for you,' she said.

Because the reason she was able to tell that story that night was because the previous night I had told it to her because the day before that her mother, who'd been visiting, had told it to me. Sooz had shown me how to tell a story - you know how it goes, so just get up there, open your mouth and do it!

The following month, when the Shaggy Dogs met again that's exactly what I did. Somehow, by the third month I'd remembered another scrap of story that I could elaborate into a ten-minute piece. Obviously, in the beginning, Alan would put me on first (new kid, if he's rubbish I can put so-and-so on afterwards to save the evening) but month by month Alan began to put me on later, then last to finish the night. Visiting tellers started giving me encouraging feedback and, when that beginner's course came around, there I was, taking part. No, I hadn't found the money. Alan told me that they had won a grant from Arts Council England to finance the course and so they were in position to offer me a free place. The course was brilliant. It was fun, practical and transformative. Then Alan and Christine started taking me to their gigs so that I could learn by listening. They started nudging me on stage,[5] 'Oh Giles, do you remember that song that so and so used to introduce that story? Well, I'm going to tell the story but I can't remember the song. Can you help me by ...'

Then Alan programmed a night of up and coming talent, and he picked me as one of three storytellers. I was elated. Later that same year, the Festival at the Edge (FATE), one of the largest storytelling festivals in the UK, contacted Alan. They wanted to programme some up and coming talent at their next festival. They were consulting certain local club promoters to ask for their recommendations and Alan recommended me. This was less than a year from when Sooz had astonished me by showing me how to tell a story. Of course, I accepted and, as the year progressed, every month, after I'd told a story in the open spot, Alan would phone me, give me meticulous, detailed and constructive feedback on what I'd done well, on what I could improve and, with his and Christine's help, I did improve.

I performed in the up and coming slot at Festival at the Edge and felt like I'd played Vegas. Early the following year, my apprenticeship still very much under way, Festival at the Edge contacted me and offered me a full booking at their next festival. I would share an hour with an experienced teller providing stories for children. I would co-host a story round (don't worry, I was told, there'll be another teller there to help you), I would do some fireside telling one evening and I was to do an hour of storytelling on my own.

An hour! I needed a set! I didn't have one and I couldn't read one! But I remembered I had a book at my childhood home, a large, illustrated book of Viking myths that I'd read and reread as a 12-year-old. My parents posted it to me. By this time I had been awarded a grant from a charity, Electronic Aids for the Blind, which paid for a computer programme that I could use to scan text or, page by page, entire books and then, after a slow and arduous conversion process (smartphones do this instantly now) I could close my eyes and listen as a computerised voice read me the Norse myths. So I began working on my set.

To assist my preparations, Alan suggested and arranged opportunities for me to practise a full-length solo performance. He arranged for me to take forty-five-minute slots, unpaid, in storytelling clubs locally, in Manchester and Lancaster. He drove me to these clubs, helped familiarise me with strange surroundings, listened to me perform and then, on the journey back, he gave me meticulous, detailed and constructive feedback on what I'd done well and on what I should next focus on to improve. I will never forget this generosity from club promoters, from FATE, from the Shaggy Dogs and, above all, from Alan Sparkes. It was, literally, life changing.

Overview

So, what about your apprenticeship? This book is intended for parents, grandparents, teachers and carers who want to actively engage their children's imagination and help them to develop aspects of their personality such as confidence with words, such as imagination, such as empathy. The course laid out in this book can also be used by teachers to get children to quickly make up, rehearse and perform exciting new stories, then recruit that excitement and investment and use it to help children through the harder task of writing their ideas down. All the exercises in this book have been used many times with classes of children and young people from 4-17 years old. Or perhaps you're a traditional storyteller? Fantastic - the structural analysis of story in this book will help sharpen your storytelling skills as you get better at learning the crucial bits quicker. They will improve your composition skills too, fine-tuning your sense of narrative. I've also used these techniques with high-ranking business people, management and C-Suite, but that's another story. This book will help with all of these things but - *important note* - in order to learn to do something fast you must be prepared to learn slow. You will notice changes and improvements in your storytelling skills with every new exercise, but please be prepared to go through every exercise thoroughly, developing your skills and confidence before you read on. You can't just arrive at the end. The journey is important.

The first thing you will do is create one story and then we will be able to use this one story as a lab, exploring it in many different ways, applying numerous techniques of creation and performance. We should do this *before* we move on to exploring all the Nine Forms of Story and the Four Types of Plot. The idea is that, having been so thorough in the creation of one story, you will already be well on your way to calling up these skills spontaneously at any moment to serve any moment.

Throughout this book it will be perfectly possible for you to read quickly through the pages, scanning each exercise, saying to yourself, 'Ok, I get that, I'll do that later.' You will finish the book fast and learn little. This book is meant to help you acquire not conceptual understanding (fast) but practical skills (slow), and skills can only be learned by doing and doing again. If you have children, or work with children, you will have seen how, in early years, they play. We use the word 'play' to describe adults who are not really trying their best but 'play', for children, is an intensely committed activity. I would like you to play at the exercises in this book as a child plays, with intensity, focus, commitment. Above all, be prepared to fail. There is no grievous failure in this book except failure to try. It's meant to be fun. The more you attempt, the more fun it is. Above all, the things you will attempt in this book are natural and instinctive. You already do them; I'm just working with you to help you do them better. So throw yourself in and dare to fail, because daring to fail is the surest route to success.

Lastly, in this book you will find, for each Form of Story, an example story. These stories are all drawn from traditional sources and have been composed following the numbered stages of each of the Forms of Story. They are meant for your pleasure as well as illustration of the Forms. But most of them are *not* directly suitable for children younger than 14, so please don't read anything to children without reading it through first! I've done this on purpose - I don't want you to read my written versions of spoken stories to children - I want you to tell your own versions in your own words.

Story and the Study of Story

Once upon a time, a woman or a man opened their mouth to tell the first ever story and, for the first time, that hush fell. Or maybe, it wasn't in our time, nor our parents', nor our grandparents', nor our great, great, great grandparents' parents' time (but it was a good time, a fine time, when ducks spoke rhyme and monkeys chewed tobacco). Or maybe, a long, long time ago, in a place that is miles from here and years from now (though it is near at hand and only a breath away), it did and it did not happen that there was and there was not a person who began something that had already started, who jumped into a stream that was already flowing, yet, however it was, they spoke, and their words were the world's first story. Stories worldwide start with openings that, in different ways, invite the listener to enter another world; a world that, at the exact same time is real and unreal. However it was that it first happened, and how-ever-so-many ways there are to start a story, somewhere, some once, by someone, the world's first story started. It is still being told.

There are different ideas about where humanity itself started. There are different ideas about how speech started, which was the first language, and there are many different theories about how many stories there are and where they originated.

For example, the Brothers Grimm, Wilhelm and Jacob, published their first anthology of stories for children in 1812. The Brothers Grimm are often described as storytellers. As far as I know, they were no such thing. They were academics, linguists, folklorists, they were collectors and writers-down of stories. Thanks to them we have 'The Frog Prince', 'Cinderella', 'Hansel and Gretel', 'Rumpelstiltskin', 'Snow White' and many more.

Except they sourced some of their stories, 'Cinderella', for example, 'Sleeping Beauty' and 'Little Red Riding Hood', from the writings of Charles Perrault (1628–1703), who is credited with inventing the fairy tale (at least in its written form). Yet all the stories he wrote down already existed as spoken word stories. Perrault wrote down his version of a version of 'Cinderella' that he happened to hear. Had he gone to a different village, or the same village on a different occasion, might the story we all know as 'Cinderella' be different? Might, for example, the fairy godmother have been a kindly vixen? Or might she have gone to the ball not in a pumpkin but a melon? We do know, for example, that the glass slipper we all *know* the prince had to fit on the correct foot was actually made of fur, and that Cinderella has had to dance in glass shoes as a result of confusion between the English word 'fur' with the French word '*verre*'. Worldwide, there are reckoned to be 3,000 versions of a story recognisable as 'Cinderella' in which a prince, for example, seeks the owner of a glass slipper, or a tin nose ring, or...

The point here is that stories move from teller to teller, place to place, culture to culture, language to language, and they have been doing so for centuries, long before scholars and linguists got involved. They have changed with every telling. Writers pen down stories like naturalists pin down butterflies, so that they can be studied. But, pinned down, they've stopped flying, or at least, that version has. The writer gets credited with having invented something they merely wrote down and anyone telling the story differently is told they're telling it 'wrong'. That version, written by an author, has become 'author-itative', the definitive version of that story.

So, Geoffrey Chaucer (1343-1400), in his *Canterbury Tales*, has his pilgrims tell stories which we may think of as English folk stories, but many of which he learned from Boccaccio (1313-75), who collected them from his native Italy. Somewhere, beneath all these versions of versions, lies an original tale, a first version. But where, when and what?

This is what Wilhelm and Jacob Grimm were looking for. As linguists, they were aware of the idea that all European and Indian languages have a common ancestor, Indo-European. No one really knows what Indo-European sounded like, what its words or its grammar exactly were. Its very existence is assumed from the way that many Indian and European languages share words with the same or related meanings, which share the same or related sounds. It existed as one language, it is inferred, because once, a very long time ago, before these people split off to become Indians, and these to be Greeks or Italians or Germans or Britons, we were one small clump of humanity. It may be true. The Brothers Grimm reckoned that if there was once one language then once there must have been only one story, the ancestor of all other stories. So when they wrote down versions of the stories they read in Perrault or heard in childhood from their nanny (French), they were looking for the evidence of that one story, that mono-myth. Rumour has it that they changed the stories they recorded to better support their hypothesis. Researchers changing evidence to support their hypothesis? That in itself is an old story.

Other writers also began making collections of stories to support an idea of nationhood. The idea, tempting and seductive, is that 'these stories are uniquely of this people, they are the special creation and property of this people'. So, in Norway, in 1841, two friends, Asbjørnsen and Moe (a schoolteacher and a minister) decided to collect Norwegian stories from the people living in the valleys and mountains of Norway inspired, in part, by a growing sense of national identity (Norway did not become fully independent from Denmark until 1905). Coming from such secluded communities, cut off from their countrymen (let alone the world) by mountains, cut off from their neighbours by snow, there are many features of Norwegian storytelling that seem unique to Norway. Except they're not, because you find them in Scotland, and (small surprise) in Orkney, Shetland and the Hebrides, which were ruled by a Norwegian king for centuries. Clearly some Norwegian stories left the dales and sailed to the islands, but who can say the same thing didn't happen the other way round? Well, it did. Asbjørnsen and Moe's excellent collection is called *East of the Sun, West of the Moon*. The title story is a glorious adventure with love, courage, magic, trolls, so very Norwegian. Except it is actually a Norwegianised version of 'Eros and Psyche', a Greek myth. And before it was Greek, what was it? People will keep going to places, meeting other people and talking with them, which is terribly inconvenient to those keen on classification ...

So it seems that no one culture can definitively claim to be the originator of this or that tale, though many people will have tried to do so on behalf of this or that culture. It seems that when studying stories you can study the things that make things special by their difference or you can study what makes things special by their commonality. If you think this is all a bit of a pickle, it is. But the good news is, for you? No one can ever tell you that you are telling a story 'wrong'. Your version differs from their version, that's all.

But you can tell a story well and you can tell a story badly. Follow the procedures in this book and you will learn to tell a story well, every time.

 Storymaking Games – Nursery Slopes

So let's start! At this point, I wish to introduce you to some games you can play with children on journeys or during long waits that will work to develop the memory of both children and yourself, also your ability to remember things in sequence by means of the connections between them. These are crucial skills in storytelling. 'Winding and Unwinding' and 'Fortunately/Unfortunately' are great creative 'limbering up' exercises as they also show how inspiration comes in that moment when you, not knowing what you are going to say, nonetheless commit to the moment and open yourself up to it. When you need inspiration it comes, and committing to that moment makes you need it. These storymaking games will lead into the Forms of Story and, if you do these first, you'll be off to a great start.

Nursery Slopes 1: Winding and Unwinding

Winding and Unwinding is a simple word association game, great for car journeys, etc. One person starts by saying a word, next person says a word they associate with the previous word, or simply inspired by it, and so on. This part of the game is called Winding and this is the easy part.

At a certain point (a point that can be extended as you all get better at the game), the person who started the game announces that it is time to start Unwinding. Now you have to start working backwards retrieving, in order, the words that precede each other. For an easier version, the order of speech can also reverse, so you end up retrieving words you yourself said. To make it harder the order of speech remains the same, so players have to remember words that other people contributed, not what they themselves said. Retrieve words originally spoken by another? Well, that sounds like storytelling to me. Give it a try.

Was that fun? Good - now you're ready for the next-level collaborative storymaking game, a game you can play with young people and which will also develop the skills in memory and a connection that will help you on your journey.

Nursery Slopes 2: Fortunately/Unfortunately

The purpose of this book, put simply, is to take you through a practical and progressional course, one in which you will learn how to successfully make up and tell brilliant stories using simple numbered structures that you will also learn how to memorise. You will learn how to improvise in the way that a jazz musician improvises, in that your flights of fancy will be grounded in a tested structure that provides scaffolding for your imagination to build on. Or you can think of the story structures as a kind of mental trellis that supports the growing, the flowering, of your creativity. You will learn how to 'conjure up' a gripping, compelling story as if from nothing. Now you might be thinking, 'Unfortunately, I'm no good at imagining and I can't magic a story out of thin air!' Fortunately, you can, and it isn't quite from thin air. You might be thinking, 'Unfortunately, you don't know me and I know I can't do it!' Fortunately, though I don't know you, I have, over the last two decades, worked with probably thousands of clients of different ages, different backgrounds, in different contexts and countries and all with different aims (some have been schoolteachers, some middle, senior management, some chief executives). I have met many people who say they can't make things up and I have never yet met one who really couldn't.

So now this is a very simple game that can be played in pairs or in groups and will enable anyone to spontaneously create a functional story. You may already know the game and you may already have guessed what it is. Do you know a game called Fortunately/Unfortunately? When I was a child we used to play it on car journeys. It made dull journeys exciting! More recently, I've used it with creatively shy children and adults as a way of limbering up their imaginations and ensuring that everyone makes a contribution.

How does it work? One person starts by making a short statement that *must* begin with the word 'Fortunately ...' The next person must follow with a statement that is connected to the first statement, but which *must* begin with the word 'Unfortunately ...'

Grab a child or bother your partner and have a go now. I'll give you an example:

Fortunately, Elliot was picked for the football team.
Unfortunately, he had no boots!
Fortunately, the game wasn't until Saturday.
Unfortunately it was Friday!
Fortunately, the shops were still open.
Unfortunately, Elliot had no money.
Fortunately, his father did.
Unfortunately, his father was still at work.
Fortunately, it was nearly five o'clock.
Unfortunately, Elliot's dad was away working in America!
Fortunately, Elliot was in America too!
Unfortunately, the football game was in Stockport.

So, I didn't pre-plan that (no, really?) but the basic structure, by and of itself sets up expectations and, as soon as you have expectations you can create twists. When it looks like it is going one way, you can send it somewhere else. This is the simplest technique for keeping an audience engaged in a story, basically by changing direction. Bear this in mind the next time you watch/listen to a soap opera or a drama serial or, for that matter, read a Charles Dickens novel - Fortunately/Unfortunately is the basic stock in trade. Many of the Forms of Story that you will meet as you move through this book have Fortunately/ Unfortunately more or less obviously coded into them. So have a go at playing Fortunately/Unfortunately now.

Did it work? Good! This is the most fundamental technique that storytelling employs, namely, the teller follows a structure from which ideas can spring spontaneously.

When playing 'Fortunately/Unfortunately' with people who are creatively shy (of all ages) I have sometimes found people play safe and simply reverse things such as:

Unfortunately, Elliot didn't have any boots.
Fortunately, he did have some boots.

This is a cop out. If you're playing this with kids, gently insist they have another go because people *do* get better with practice. I began using this game with a group of young blind students who were very timid and used this cop out a lot. I let them, for a bit, and then said, 'That's good but I'm sure we can do better ...' Little by little they did get better, then much better. So do it again.

Better? Good. Now read on ...

The Forms of Story

I said at the start of this book that the techniques we'll explore together are derived from the study and analysis of traditional story. I think it better to base analysis on traditional stories because traditional stories have been edited over centuries, sometimes millennia, by the harshest editor in the world - forgetfulness. Over time the weaker bits have been forgotten and the best bits passed on. These best bits are the forms I have found by comparing and studying the stories, hundreds of them, that I have in my head. I've had to do it in my head because I've been registered blind since 2000 and for at least twelve years I was completely unable to access the printed word. I learned storytelling by listening. So, how many types of story are there?

The answer to this question will again depend on who you ask. I have already mentioned how the Brothers Grimm thought, at root, there was only one story, and you could say that all stories feature a character who, in the course of the story, struggles to overcome a problem. All stories, therefore, are the same story, the story of humanity's struggle to survive against the odds. Probably true, but a bit vague, don't you think? What other ideas are there on the subject? Or what versions of that struggle?

The great Ancient Greek philosopher Aristotle wrote that all stories must contain a beginning, a middle and an end. You probably heard that at primary school. It's true, but a bit meaningless, because all he's really said is that a story starts, goes on a bit, and then stops. This is probably not the kind of thinking that has made Aristotle so famous. Many primary schools in the United Kingdom nowadays use something called the Story Mountain, which dictates there must be a start, then rising action, then falling action and then the end. Better, yes, but still a bit vague? We'll come back to this later when we explore the arc of a story. For now, Story Mountain still seems a bit sparse.

At the other end of the scale you have the Aarne-Thompson-Uther Index. First published in 1910, but added to and reissued, the taxonomy of folktales known as ATU enumerates distinct types of folk tale, grouping them not by structure but by motifs or incidents common across stories, such as swords being drawn from stones or oak trees, heroes made invulnerable apart from a fatal weak spot (the heel, between the shoulder blades, kryptonite, a weakness for Jaffa Cakes), mysterious companions who help young men to their fortune then disappear, magical animals, talking horses, etc. Aarne-Thompson narrows it down to only two thousand-plus types of folktale. Too much? Don't worry – Vladimir Propp (1895–1970), who published his *Morphology of the Folktale* in 1928, analysed the structure of Russian folktales and broke them down into just thirty-one functions. I'm guessing these numbers seem a little intimidating? Isn't there anything simpler?

There is. Perhaps you've heard the theory that there are only seven stories? That sounds a bit more manageable, I hope? This theory claims that all stories everywhere will fit into one of the following seven story structure categories:

1. The Quest
2. Journey and Return
3. Rags to Riches
4. Rebirth
5. Discovering the Monster
6. Comedy
7. Tragedy

That probably makes sense, seems familiar, right? As we go forward our work will be based on these seven structures, plus two more, so nine story structures in total. Unlike the original proponents of this theory, or the proponents of many of the others, I do not claim this list is exhaustive, complete, definitive or even 'true'. There may be many more, indeed, I hope there are because I'd love to learn them. What I do know is that I have used these story structures hundreds of times to help children, adults, businesses, museums, more, to quickly create new stories and, whether or not they're true or exhaustive, they work. They will work for you too if you work with them. It is not necessary that every story you create should conform *exactly* to these Forms of Story. It's OK to shift from one to the other, taking a bit from here, a bit from there, and for the character you primarily focus on to shift as the tale goes on, but, certainly while you are learning, the closer you can stick to these structures the more assured your results will be. In my own practice, I have worked with ancient source materials (Irish wonder tale, Icelandic saga) and, finding myself unsatisfied with the written version I'm using, I have looked for the story structure beneath a given version. Having identified which structure it is closest to, I have *sharpened* things where I feel they have got vague or muddled. It works; the tale flows better and makes more sense to listeners.

Memory I: Building Your Palace

Building Your Memory

How good is your memory? How much do you even use it nowadays? How much do you rely on a smartphone to do your remembering for you? A tablet? Pen and paper? Probably quite a lot. Except these items don't help you remember things. Quite the opposite; they help you forget. Because, once you write something down you no longer need to remember it, and you don't remember them, but you do remember to look at your list. You have effectively and efficiently outsourced your memory to what becomes an extension of your brain and as long as you remember to look at it, it works. But what if you forget to do that? Or you lose it? And what becomes of your capacity to remember things if you underuse it in this way?

Memory, for most people, is predominantly visual, but ultimately it works with all your senses. Smells are evocative of memory, the body has memory, sounds will 'ring a bell'. How can you use your memory better?

The good news is that it's easy! Let's learn how to build your Memory Palace.

Your Memory Palace

If you watch British TV you probably already know what this is, though you may not know you do. Sherlock Holmes (as played by Benedict Cumberbatch) uses a Memory Palace in a way that (and this always happens!) reimagines ancient techniques in the guise of contemporary technology. So, when struggling with a conundrum, Holmes is shown flipping through a bewildering slide show of mental images with the speed of a processor chip until he reaches his 'Aha!'

moment. Not bad for a character born before the computer. But Memory Palaces are real and can be used to achieve prodigious feats of recollection. The mentalist Derren Brown uses a Memory Palace to simultaneously count four complete packs of cards in order to beat the house in casinos. The good news for casinos is that, although knowing how to do this is simple, doing it is not - it takes tremendous effort, practise and talent. Luckily, using a Memory Palace for storytelling is much easier.

The first historically known use of Memory Palace goes back to Marcus Tullius Cicero (106-43 BC). Cicero was a lawyer, philosopher, rhetorician and politician in Ancient Rome and was famous, still is, for being the greatest public speaker of his age. Cicero's speeches could change the actions of the entire Roman Empire. He rose to be Consul of Rome (the head of state) on the strength of this speech making and he did it all without a slide projector or PowerPoint. As Cicero himself said, 'Power corrupts. PowerPoint corrupts pointlessly!'[6] He spoke at length to large crowds in the Forum of Rome or in the Senate, and he spoke confidently without the use of notes. Somebody once asked him how he was able to speak at such length and in such detail without the use of notes and he asked his questioner if they had noticed that, as he spoke, he moved around the Forum, delivering one section of his speech by this column, another by that column? The questioner said yes, they had noticed, and wasn't that to make sure all parts of the audience felt included? Cicero said that was partly the case, but it was also how he remembered his speeches.

Cicero used the Forum of Rome as his Memory Palace. He explained that, when he was memorising his speech he would make images that would remind him of particular sections of his speech and, in his mind, 'place' them at this or that column. Then, as he spoke, when he moved to this or that column, the appropriate part of his speech would appear in his mind. Brilliant, right? And the good news for you is that what you have to do is far, far simpler.

Because you don't need to memorise facts, data or complex sections of a speech. You can, of course, use these techniques to do just that, and I teach my business students to do so, but that is not the focus of this book. You only need to make Memory Palaces to memorise, permanently, the handful of words that will guide you confidently through the spontaneous creation of a cracking story. I've noticed, when I'm working with students, that Memory Palace helps them build the memory. When I test them a week later they can quickly, confidently, accurately recall items without actually using the Memory Palace. It's done its work and the memory is distributed in the mind. So let's start now.

1

The Quest: Six-Part Story and Hero's Journey

The Quest

Let's start with the Quest. You're on a quest yourself, after all, to become a great storyteller. We can create our first story together and, in the process, learn how to make a Memory Palace. Having learned it once, you can use the same Memory Palace to memorise the eight other Forms of Story that you will need as we go further into your storytelling journey.

What is the Quest?

The Quest is a story about a character, or sometimes characters, who, of their own free will, choose to embark on a difficult and dangerous journey on which they overcome great challenges in order to solve the problem that prompted their quest in the first place. This is usually for the sake of other people. *The Odyssey* is a Quest. *The Lord of the Rings* and every Bond movie you've ever seen are Quests. 'Theseus and the Minotaur' is a Quest, as is *The Voyage of the Argo* and *Raiders of the Lost Ark*. The original *Star Wars* film (now called *Episode 4*) is a Quest.

Actually, one of the reasons that that first *Star Wars* film has been so successful is that it was closely based on the essential structure of the Quest, and that's no fluke. In 1949 an American anthropologist called Joseph Campbell wrote a superb work of comparative mythology, *The Hero with the Thousand Faces*. The influence of this book has been, and continues to be, immense. Campbell studied hero myths from all over the world and picked out the elements that occurred repeatedly in different hero stories from different cultures. In other words, he studied the things which made them the same. He boiled these down to just eight elements. The original *Star Wars* screenplay follows these eight steps faithfully. The result? Well, it's done all right, hasn't it?

Two Israeli psychotherapists, Ofra Ayalon and Mooli Lahad, distilled this structure even further, boiling it down to something they call the Six-Part Story Process. Your Quest is going to follow these six steps and, as you meet them, you will simultaneously learn to remember them.

So, start by choosing the exact location of your Memory Palace. Call to your mind a location such as a building or a landscape with permanent features. This place should be somewhere you know very well, and one that you can clearly imagine walking round in a particular, and repeatable, sequence. It needs to have an entrance and at least six rooms. You only need an entrance and five rooms for this, but you will need more later. It might be a home you know or knew – I use the house I grew up in. It might be a school, a college, somewhere you've worked, it might be a public park, a valley or farm, but wherever it is, you know it well enough to picture it clearly and have for it, also, a logical order in which you would walk round it. Don't read on until you've done this.

Got it? Good. Now take a walk in your mind through your chosen location.

Now we learn how to turn that remembered location into a powerful Memory Palace. To do this you are going to create images in response to prompts I will give you and place them first at the entrance and afterwards in each of the rooms, or specific, separately knowable locations, in turn. Then, in your mind, you can walk around your Memory Palace and, when you find the image you put in place there, it will bring to your mind the thing you needed to remember. It is important that these images be memorable, so make your images as rich and interesting as you can, use pictures, smells, sounds, movements, sensations, anything, just so long as it's whatever *you* need. I once worked with a totally blind student who obviously didn't use pictures when he imagined things – he told me he used sensations under his hands. Use whatever works best for you.

1) The First Location, the Entrance. Here you must place an image that will make you remember the words 'Who' and 'Where'.

An example to help you start: the image I use is *Doctor Who*, mad eyes and madder hair, standing at the door of my parents' house staring in confused desperation at a map that he is turning round and around as he tries to work out Where he is. If you didn't grow up in Britain in the 1970s, this specific image might not help you much. I apologise. UK or not, it is important you find your own image. Do this now.

2) The Second Location (which might be a room, the hall, a different field or hill, I don't know. I can't see your Memory Palace). Here, create and put in place a powerful image that will make you remember the word 'Problem'.

3) The Third Location. Here, place a powerful image that will make you remember the word 'Journey'.

4) The Fourth Location. Place an image here that will make you remember the words 'Friend/Help'.

5) The Fifth Location. Place an image here that will make you remember the words 'Enemy/Obstacle'.

6) Place an image here that will make you remember the word 'Conclusion'.

Done? That's great. Now close your eyes and take a walk through your Memory Palace, taking time to stop at each location, meeting the image you put there and calling to mind the exact words the image was created to remind you of.

Done? Good. Now take a pen and paper (or whatever you take notes on). Go round your Memory Palace again and write down each word in the order your Memory Palace evokes.

Done? Good. Now read on. Does your list say:

The Quest Checklist

1. Who and Where
2. Problem
3. Journey
4. Friend/Help
5. Enemy/Obstacle
6. Resolution

Did it work? That's wonderful! Not quite? Don't worry, this is only the first time you've tried to accomplish a new task.

Go back and do it again. Next, we can work on creating a story.

Memory II – Sleep on it

But before we start work on your story, I'd like to share another memory technique. Sleep on it.

More than likely, you can't simply take a nap right now, but tonight, when you're getting ready to sleep, go through your Memory Palace and the Quest last thing. Tomorrow morning, I guarantee, you will find it easy to remember each element. I learned this from experience. I told you how, years ago, I was working hard to learn one hour's worth of Norse myths for my first ever booking as a featured teller at the Festival at the Edge storytelling festival. The stories were going in just fine, I could easily remember what happened, but the names of characters, artefacts and places kept escaping me. The names no doubt all had clear meanings in Old Norse and therefore clear and memorable connections to the things they were the names of, but to me they were just strange and abstract words and I couldn't make them stick in my mind. In sheer frustration I took a nap. When I awoke I realised I could now remember every name easily, and sleep had moved things from my working memory to my long-term memory.

I've since had this effect corroborated by cognitive specialists. Apparently, when a thing is in your working memory it sits in the frontal lobes of your brain. When a thing has moved to long-term memory, apparently it's really hard to see any one specific place where it is stored but using functional magnetic resonance image scanning, scientists can see the same memory being retrieved at the same time from different places in the brain. In other words, it has been distributed. This is amazing as it suggests that, were we to suffer damage to a part of our brain, certain memories have more chance of surviving because they are not stored in one but in many places, like external backup for your computer. So, if you need to remember something, think about it hard, then sleep on it. It really works.

Creating Your First Story

So, now we are going to conjure a story out of thin air. It will take only six minutes. We are not going to use a piece of paper or anything to take notes on. We are going to use a timer, set to alarm after sixty seconds and we are going to use our minds. You think I'm crazy? I know I'm not.

Before we begin, some quick, simple rules:

In each stage you will make a choice. Stick to it. Do not change it later on.

Don't worry about getting the 'best idea'. You might not and it doesn't matter. At this stage, we are exploring the *process* only, to show that it works. It is much more important that you *commit* to an idea than it be a 'good' idea (whatever that is).

Don't worry about creating the 'best' story. This is the first time you've tried this method and you can only improve on something once you've done it once.[7] You will be doing this again and again, once you know how.

Stick to the sixty-second time limit for each stage. Please commit to this, because clarity comes from commitment, not the other way round.[8] Honestly, I've learned from experience that, in this process and at this stage, allowing yourself more time does not improve the result.

Please put your phone on silent and set your timer.

Ready? Start the timer, now read on ...

1) Who is Your Story About and Where are They?

When your timer ends, move on.

2) What is Your Character's Problem?

Invent a problem that faces your character. What is it?

TIP: the Problem is what drives your story. Make it a big one.

Bell gone! Please move on.

3) What is the Journey Your Character Must Undertake?

TIP: Everything else in the story now happens as a part of this Journey.

Ping! Move on.

4) Friend/Help

On the Journey they are taking to overcome their Problem, your character now encounters either someone who becomes their Friend and Helps them on their Journey or encounters something that is helpful to them. Who or what is it?

Decided? Great. Please move on.

5) Enemy/Obstacle

Next, your Character meets someone or something who (or which) acts as an Enemy to them, or encounters an Obstacle that makes their Journey harder. Who or what is it?

The bell has rung for the final lap. Please move on ...

6) Resolution

How does your story end? Does your character overcome their Enemy/Obstacle and solve their Problem? Or is the Enemy too strong, the Problem too difficult? Success or failure? Happy or sad ending? You choose ...

That's it! You've created a Quest story! Now, in your mind only and without making written notes, go back to the start of your story and run through it out loud. Please do this **three** times.

 The Bones

You have now found what storytellers call 'the bones' of your story. These are the irreducible elements without which the story cannot function. These are the elements that Joseph Campbell had the genius to go looking for in *The Hero with the Thousand Faces*. What you have come up with, whatever its individual and unique elements, has the structure of a Quest story and will work as one. Even just in bones form it flows, it captures, it holds and moves a listener's attention. Well done. The next task is to start putting some flesh on those bones ...

But before we leave the bones entirely, a little game to test them and to test you.

Testing the Bones

From a deck of cards take cards from any suit numbered ace to six. If you don't own a deck of cards (I don't) write numbers on six Post-it notes or bits of paper. A dice won't work for this game, because we don't want the same number to come up more than once.

On your own, or you could devolve choice to a partner, shuffle up the numbers and then pick them or have them presented to you in a randomised order.

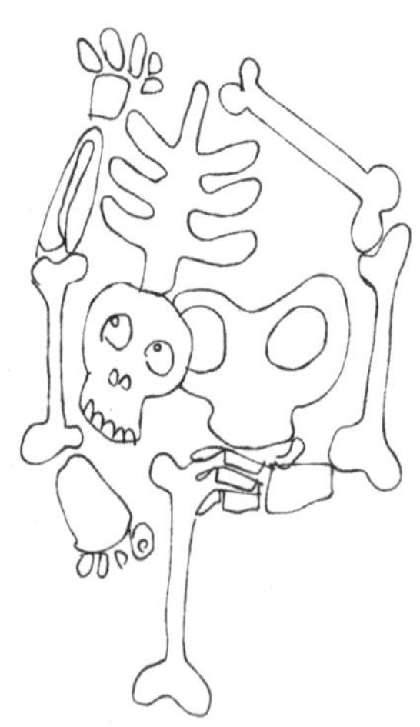

Whatever number you get, start telling your story immediately from that point, and I mean 'tell'! Speak it out loud, commit to that. It's so easy to cheat if you just do it in your head. When you're ready, pick again, or indicate that you are ready for the next number. And here is a tip from an experienced storyteller – what? You've got no idea what to say? Wonderful! Just start talking, keeping in mind which section of the structure you are in and the clarity will come as you talk. It's exciting. You already know the ideas – how are you going to connect them?

So, how did that feel? How well did it work? Were you able to make new connections, transitions, segues? Good! This is where the magic of storytelling really starts to happen, not so much in the ideas themselves but in the way in which you, the storyteller, link them, connect them. So shuffle your prompts and do it again, in different order as directed by your cards/notes, twice more. Have fun realising how, though the order is different each time, it remains the same story.

The Arc of a Story – Freitag's Triangle

As you ran through your story, even in bones form, did you feel the intensity changing? As in, does it seem to build to a certain point, getting more exciting, and then afterwards release some of that tension? I'm hoping it did.

Because there is an arc to a story, a shape by which it builds tension, reaches a peak and then releases tension. Think about a Bond movie or any thriller – there comes a point of maximum emotional intensity and dramatic excitement, often where the hero or heroine is trapped in the clutches of the evil genius, who smugly explains how horribly the main character is going to die. The main character almost never does and we know that they won't. We've seen movies like this before, but still we buy in and still we get excited.

The film never ends at this point, this pitch of excitement. Whatever the film is, after the peak of excitement there's a coming down, hence in *Star Wars* (the original) there's a medal ceremony and lots of people and aliens smiling. In Bond films it used to be that the film closed with Bond, who has escaped certain death and saved the world a couple of scenes earlier, being cheeky to his bosses before turning his attention to the beautiful woman in his arms/bed/rocket/jacuzzi/speedboat. This woman is the lucky one because, unlike the woman seduced in the first third of the movie, she doesn't end up dead in the next scene (and yet this surviving heroine seldom makes it to the next movie). See how much we like to repeat an effective story structure? This arc is not only something we expect; it's something we require and our sense of satisfaction with a story depends on our requirements being fulfilled.

Remember the Story Mountain technique I mentioned earlier that lots of British schoolteachers use to help children create stories? Well, it is built into the Six-Part Story Process, the Quest structure. It's built into the story you just created in just six minutes.

Aristotle analysed Greek Tragedy, plays adapted from traditional oral storytelling. Gustav Freytag (nineteenth-century German novelist and playwright) analysed Greek and Shakespearian Tragedy and made a neat image which is the basis of the Story Mountain used in early education. Here it is:

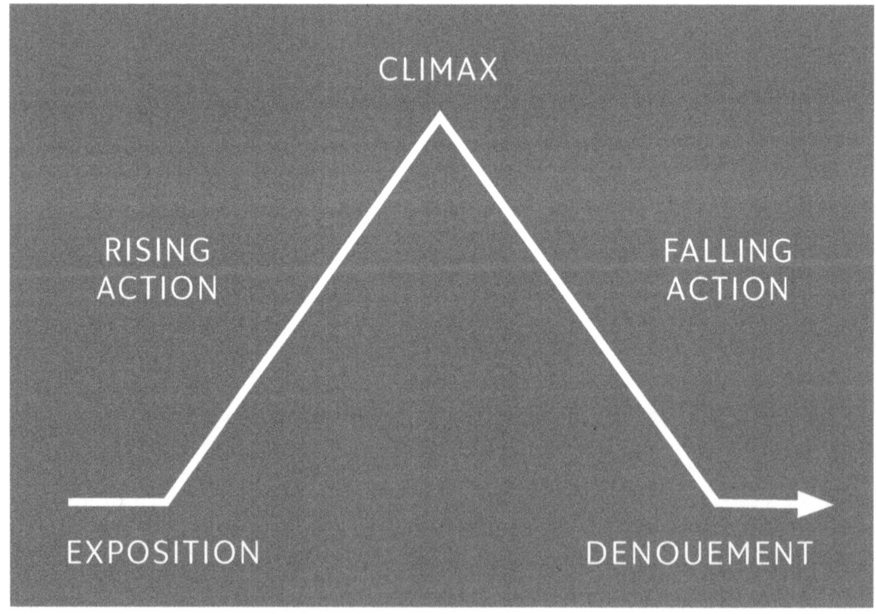

But look at where the emotional peak happens. If we take the horizontal axis to be the timeline of the story, we reach the emotional peak halfway through and have an entire half of the story/play/film to follow. However, in your Quest story the peak of excitement comes not at Stage 3 but at Stage 5, 'Enemy/Obstacle', right? So, the arc of a story should look more like this:

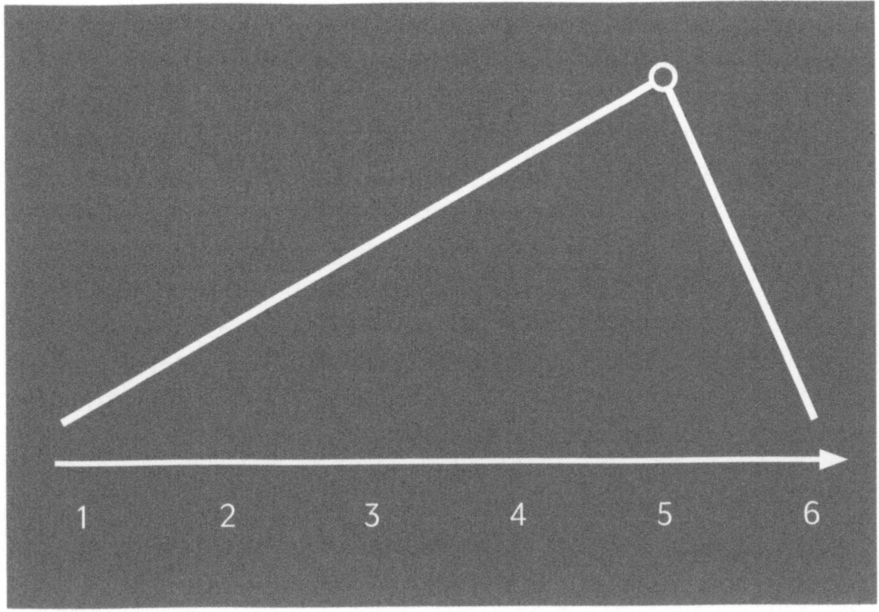

In modern thriller movies, Elizabethan English and Ancient Greek Tragedies, as well as countless traditional myths, this is exactly the arc a story is expected to follow. It would feel 'wrong' if it didn't.

Putting Flesh on the Bones

So now you've conjured a story out of thin air, you've told it once in the order in which it came to you and you've told it again and again, three times and in differing sequences. If you haven't, do, before you read on. The words change from telling to telling, and it even 'happens' in a different sequence, but it remains the same story. This is the secret of the persistence of great stories; they can change and change, pass from teller to teller, language to language, from words to pictures to music to film to computer game to words and, though they change, at their core, they remain the same story. You've also learned the arc of a story. You've noticed how knowing the steps of a story structure helps you remember where you are while 'conjuring a story out of thin air' and, most importantly, helps you know where you have to get to next. This simultaneous awareness of where you are and where you're going is vital in fluent storytelling.

There's more we can do. Before we go on to explore eight more Forms of Story that you will be able to use to conjure up great, exciting stories, we are going to spend more time on the Quest. Our own particular quest is to journey together through the process of taking the bones and fleshing them out into a fully crafted, satisfying story. This will not be instant but it will be surprisingly fast and, once you've learned these techniques, you can apply them to each of the other Forms of Story that you will meet as we go through this book. With practise you will even learn how to apply them instantly.

Because now it's time to take the bones of your story and add more flesh, to really shape and craft your story. You have, by now, already told the bones of your story some four times and the tale is getting quite grooved in. A few more repetitions and you will be absolutely confident of your material and, here's the cool thing, it really is *your* material.

So now we are going to play some games to explore what kind of language you can use when telling a story. Remember, we are going to play, but not in the way that adults mean 'play', which is to say without commitment (oh, they're only *playing* at it ...). We are going to play the way that children play, with total commitment and engagement. This is one of the reasons children learn so much so fast. Ready to play like a child?

For this section you will find it easier if you have a partner to play with. If you haven't then you'll have to use your imagination. These next few games will pull your story around, mess it up a bit. Don't worry. It's worth it. You're about to learn, through experience, how best to balance different elements of language in your telling. Once you've had a good chance to explore them with someone else's help, you'll be able to apply these techniques in the moment, on the fly, without anyone's help. The stories that you magic are about to get much more magical.

 Detail

Get a partner to sit opposite you. You will tell, they will disrupt, challenge, provoke you, not for the pleasure of it but to help you make your story better. Got someone in mind? This doesn't have to be another adult – I have run countless sessions in which children of 5+ have been able to perform this exercise effectively and meaningfully.

The following instructions are for both you the storyteller and your partner:

> Partner – your role is to challenge the storyteller for more detail. When you hear a phrase, clap your hands, ask a very brief question focussed on what you want to hear more detail about. For example, perhaps the storyteller just told you that a car came down the road. What more do you want to know? Perhaps 'how wide?'
>
> Storyteller – you are telling a story, not having a conversation, so don't answer the question directly. Instead, rephrase what you have just said but in a way which answers your partner's question so, perhaps, 'a car came down a wide road ...'
>
> Partner – what else do you want to know? 'What time?' 'What colour?' 'How fast?' Now your storyteller should be saying something like, 'It was early morning, and a red car came zooming down a wide road ...'

Now, is that just a little bit more engaging than 'a car came down the road'? This is one of the reasons why story can be so powerful. When telling a story, a good teller accesses, lights up, multiple areas of their brain connected with sight, sound, smell, taste, touch and emotion. When a listener listens, exactly the same parts of their brain are activated. Essentially, through sharing story, storyteller and listener create a shared brain pattern. This is why telling a story brings you so incredibly close to your child or to the children in your care, and this is why hearing a story is so good for the development of their brains.

Now you know the object and the rules of this game, let's play.

> Sit with your partner. Set a timer for five minutes. Begin your story and, as your partner claps their hands and challenges you to supply detail, maintain a clear relationship to them and to your task. You are *not* having a conversation, you are telling a story. Your story may be pulled off course. That's fine. This is an exercise, not a performance.

Partners, please experiment with:

1. Challenging your storyteller to, first of all, provide what seems the right amount of detail to make the story interesting but allowing it to keep flowing.
2. Then challenge your storyteller for more detail than you really want. This doesn't have to be rapid fire, but you need to keep asking for so much detail that the flow of the story is impeded.

Five minutes up? Good. Now, storyteller, go back to the beginning of your story and tell it through, but now the partner does not interrupt, but simply listens actively. Next, if you are truly working as partners, swap! If only one of you is working on being a storyteller, it's time to discuss:

What happened to the story as you added, in response to your partner's challenge, more detail?

What happened to the story when you were forced to add too much detail?

What happened to the story once the storyteller was allowed free rein *after* having been directed to add more detail?

Is it growing? Getting better?

I thought it would.

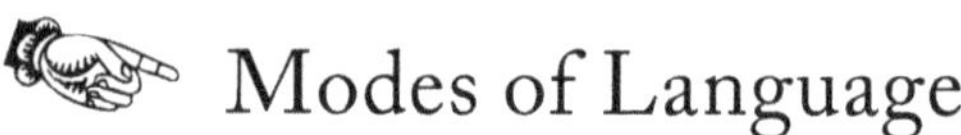

Modes of Language

After exploring detail, we are going to zoom in a little on what you have already been doing. In adding detail, you will have been changing your use of language as you told your story; specifically, you will have been moving from one predominant Mode of Language[9] to another. You will have just done it without being aware of what you did, so now we need to become conscious of our use of Modes of Language. Many people - schoolteachers, writers and writing tutors and film-makers - have written and posted about this topic. I am particularly grateful to Ben Haggarty,[10] who led a workshop I attended in the early days of my involvement with storytelling.

So what are the modes of language you can use when telling a story? Well, and perhaps this isn't a surprise to you, they are exactly the same as the Modes of Language you use when speaking in normal life, so, Action, Description and Feeling. The grammarians among you might wish to have them described as verbs (Action), adjectives and adverbs (Description and Feeling). If you're a film-maker, you might think of them as Action, Establishing Shot and Close Shot (though I know it's not quite as clear and simple as that).

Language of Action is only concerned with what somebody or something does, did or is doing. It has no business with what they look like, sound like, smell like, taste like when they are doing it and still less with how they feel while doing it. Language of Description can deal with what things, objects or places look like, sound like, smell like, taste like, feel like (feel meaning through touch, not emotion) but has nothing to do with what things are doing. Language of Feeling is only about emotion. These are the terms and categories for the next game. Clear?

Your partner is going to be in charge of which Mode of Language you are to use when telling your story. Again, children of 5+ can participate in this perfectly easily with adults or with other children as partners. Sit opposite one another. Storyteller, you are going to give control of your use of language entirely to your partner and only tell as they direct you to.

Partners, you are going to clap your hands and say one of only three words: Action! Description! Feeling!

Whichever you say, the storyteller must *instantly* begin their story using *only that Mode of Language*. If you order them to tell in Action and they start dropping in bits of Description or Feeling, clap your hands and restate your command.

Partners, when you feel that you wish to, clap your hands again, and demand a different Mode of Language. Storytellers, whatever you are saying, you must *instantaneously* change to whichever Mode of Language your partner has indicated. Your story is going to get pulled all over the place. Don't worry, this is good.

So, set a timer for five minutes and begin. Partners, please direct your storyteller to change mode when it feels right to you that they should.

Done? Good. Now time for some quick reflection. Discuss, in answer to the following questions:

What does language of Action do to a story?
What does language of Description do?
And Feeling?

When you've done this, set a timer for five minutes and make ready to begin again. Only this time, partners, who have previously been changing the Mode of Language when it felt right to do so, you are now to keep your storyteller in this or that Mode of Language for longer than feels comfortable. In fact, the less comfortable it feels, the better.

Have you explored that? Thank you! Now, I'd like you to discuss:

What happened *to the story* when you were left in language of Action too long?
What happened *to the story* when left in Description too long?
And Feeling?

One last thing, and this relates to Description and Feeling. Let me describe a scene to you:

> It's winter. It is already dark and a film of rain is pushed down the greasy pavement by a strong wind. An old man is struggling uphill towards a bus stop, his legs bent, his back crooked, his hands struggling to hold his shopping bags. In the road, a bus comes swishing past him, pauses at the bus stop at the top of the hill. The old man struggles to go faster but the bags keep banging his legs and then, suddenly, one of the carrier bags bursts and tins and cartons go bouncing and rolling down the hill. The bus pulls away. The old man looks at the trail of littered shopping and his head sinks even lower.
>
> He was sad.

Now, did I need those last three words? Or is it possible to use Description in such a way that the language of Feeling is unnecessary because the listener already *knows* how the character is feeling? If you can do that, you can make the storyteller almost vanish and the listener will simply 'see' the story in their minds as it unfolds for them. Powerful stuff.

Storytellers, now that you've been forced, by relinquishing choice to your partner, to become conscious of the modes of language you use when telling a story, please tell your story again. This time you are in charge and your partner is only to listen, to observe, but please invite something of what you've learned about the roles of Action, Description and Feeling in storytelling to influence how you now choose to tell your story by your own free will. When you're done, ask your listener and ask yourself, how is it going? Is it growing? Flowing? Improving?

When using the languages of Action, Description and Feeling in telling a story to a child or children, one fun thing to do to increase children's engagement and spark up their incredible imagination is to invite them to contribute. It's best if you keep hold of the language of Action, of the 'what happens' of your story (but you don't have to if you don't want to), but you can ask children questions like 'what do you think the ... looked like?' or 'how do you think they felt?' and then take their answers and use them in your storytelling. In this way, the story creation and telling become a shared, collaborative activity. Engagement and concentration intensify still further. At the end, you can thank them for telling the story with you and point out it wouldn't have been nearly so good without their help. This isn't flattery - it wouldn't have.

Bonus Mode of Language

There is another Mode of Language that I have held back until you'd had a good go with the basic three modes. This fourth mode is very powerful and can make or break a story. Use it right and it enhances the power of a story. Use it just a little too much and the story is ruined. What is it?

This fourth Mode of Language is the language of Comment. When you are telling a story as narrator you are not *in* the story (in the way that an actor is in a play). When you speak as a character, your character is *in* the story. We'll cover this in more detail later. Your listener is literally entranced, as their mind has entered a gentle trance, a different state of consciousness, and they are creating the story and its world in their own minds as they listen. And then you Comment on it. Squelch.

Because when you Comment on the story while you are telling it, you,have stepped in front of the story and pointed at it. Instead of speaking the story, you have said something about it. The world the listener has been creating disappears; they are suddenly back in the real world. The spell is broken as if, when you're watching a film, the camera were to pull back suddenly and show the crew, microphones, cameras and that the scene is only a set. So why would you do such a thing?

Let me give you some examples of how I might use Language of Comment. You won't need me to, but nonetheless I shall put the Comment in *italics*:

> The bear knocked on the hillside and it opened. The young woman followed the bear inside and inside it was a palace! Tapestries, carpets, sculpture, suits of armour, clearly it was a palace. Now this young woman had lived her whole life in a turf-roofed cabin. She'd never seen inside a rich farmhouse, let alone a manor house or a castle, she'd definitely never seen a palace but it must be a palace because it looked exactly like the palaces she'd heard about from Fairy Stories, *although, at her age, you'd think she was much too grown up to be taking Fairy Stories seriously* ... So she followed the Bear inside, wide-eyed with amazement ...

So, what did that little Comment, that interruption, do? I use this technique when I'm telling a fairy story to grown-ups or to young people who likely think themselves too grown up to be listening to fairy stories. Why?

In 2017 I was teaching a private client, giving him 1:1 lessons to train his speaking voice. He is a professional hypnotherapist. We discussed our different disciplines and he told me that when he is putting a client into a trance he will deliberately address some remarks to the client's rational mind, their critical mind. He does this artfully in order that, by directly addressing the critical mind and saying, 'don't worry, we both know you're here, we both know this isn't really real', he can then put the client into a deeper trance. Reassured that it is not forgotten, the critical mind feels it safe to allow the experience to continue.

So, as a storyteller you can do this too with audiences of all ages (you will know that children aged 2 have a sharp grasp of logic and illogic, of sensible and silly). Use the Language of Comment judiciously and you can deepen the experience of a story.

What happens when you use it too often? I see this time and again when I'm running storymaking workshops with adolescents. They, having fairly recently discovered the power of irony and, at the same time, the danger of (and hence fear of) commitment, will continually pepper stories with throwaway comments and muttered ironic asides. I have to tell them that most of their muttered asides are not even audible to the audience. If you keep leaving the audience out in this way (because they can't hear you, they are excluded) the audience will check out, and you won't get them back. If you keep making throwaway remarks you literally throw it away, all of it, the story, the magic, the trance, the audience's goodwill, attention, and ultimately, the audience itself. Why should they commit to listening if you can't commit to telling? How many best man speeches have you heard that did exactly this?

So, tell your story one more time, allowing yourself free choice of Action, Description, Feeling and, *sparingly*, Comment. How well does it work? Before you move on further in this book, at this point I recommend you repeat what you've done using the Quest structure so far. Make up and tell some more Quest stories: different characters, different problems and outcomes. As you do this, you may well, instinctively, start using some of the more advanced techniques we will be exploring next. This is good – storytelling is a natural and instinctive human activity. When you're ready to start consciously exploring some more facets of storymaking and storytelling, read on.

The Fear of Empty Spaces

When you've got to a level of confidence with your use of the Quest story structure, with Action, Description and Feeling and Comment, then you're ready to try something more advanced. It is time to recruit the power that springs from our fear of empty spaces.

In the 1990s I was hired to tell stories to a group of blind and visually impaired children. I mentioned this to my mother, who wondered how I could do that? After all, what could I describe that they could imagine? I answered that many of them would have some sight, as indeed I do, and that I thought they would most likely have their own relationship with words that they must hear continually in everyday speech. I trusted their imaginations to process words in ways that were meaningful to them. She was doubtful, so I began to tell her the beginning of a wonderful Irish story known as 'The Wanderings of Oisin'. I had described a group of warriors sat around brush fires at night by the shore of a lake, and then a woman appearing on the far side of the lake, mounted on a horse. The woman, I said, was so beautiful that the men stopped whatever they were doing and just looked at her. They rose to their feet, the blood thumping at their temples, their bodies leaning forwards in attitudes of expectation, each one of them willing her to come closer.

Then I asked my mother what colour that lady's hair was? 'It was golden,' she said. And the horse, what colour? 'It was white,' she said, firmly. How did she know, I asked her? 'Because you said so!' my mother said, with a tone almost of surprise at my asking such a silly question. It took some persuasion to convince her that I had deliberately said nothing of the kind, never precisely describing hair or horse.

Never forget that, as you are telling your story, your listener is simultaneously (or a fraction later) creating in their own mind their own version of your story. Their mind is aligning with yours in a process known as 'neural coupling'. If you, in your story, describe a character falling out of a tower and landing in a river, those parts of the brain that light up in somebody who really is falling out of a real tower and landing in a real river will also light up in your listener's mind as they imagine the experience. This is one of the reasons that storytelling is so vital to the development of young people – it gives, to the inexperienced, as real a sense of experience as is possible without the dangers of the actual experience.

You can use this engagement by the listener in very powerful ways when telling a story to children. One of the secrets to intensifying the power of your story lies in what you leave out.

In 2007 I was commissioned by the Festival at the Edge, a wonderful storytelling festival then held annually on Wenlock Edge in Shropshire, to create a new performance based on a traditional tale. This was to be for an adult audience. I chose, from the Ulster Cycle, *The Third Sorrow of Storytelling*, 'The Sons of Uisneach'. This story is also known as 'Deirdre of the Sorrows'. It tells of a girl who, at the moment of her birth, is foretold to become one day so beautiful as will give beauty itself a new name. So, in this whole performance (which takes more than an hour and a half), can you guess what is the one thing I never described?

I never said what she looked like. The reason is simple. If I say to any audience that this was the most beautiful woman in the world, every member of the audience will have their own idea of what that is. If I specify, I am going to ruin the story for everyone who wanted their Deirdre to look different, who didn't share my idea of what makes a woman beautiful. It's even worse if I were to allow them time to create, in their own minds, their image of Deirdre and then, later, crash their image by specifying mine. Actually, throughout my composition of that story I learned that the more I left out the better.

Why? Well, if I'm describing something to you and I give you just enough for you to be heading in the right direction, but I leave out that crucial last ingredient that will complete your picture, what are you going to do? Are you going to leave that space in your mental picture empty? Or are you going to complete it yourself? Of course, you will complete it yourself. This means you, the listener, are actively engaged in the creation of the story's world, and it is perfectly fitted to you, and then you are *inside* the story. Never forget, the audience's version of a story is more important than yours, so allow them the room to make it their own.

Theory over, how can you use this when creating a story out of thin air for children?

For a start, it's much easier with spoken than written word. But, let's imagine some moments in a story. In describing a character or scene, you might list some attributes. For example, the knight might have legs like tree trunks, a chest like a barrel and his laugh was like the boom of the sea. But you could say, 'The knight, well, he was so strong that his legs were like tree trunks, his chest was like a barrel and his laugh was ...!'

You can be artfully vague to very powerful effect. I was once telling a story to a group of 10-year-old girls at a school. They'd asked me for a scary story and I started something very simple, a silly story that I'd learned from a 9-year-old girl. It features a dead grandmother rising from the grave to come and reclaim her stolen liver from her granddaughter (9-year-olds can be very gruesome in their tastes and a story is a safe place to explore fear). As the grandmother approaches there is a refrain: 'I'm in the graveyard. I want my liver. Are you there?'

As grannie got closer, I said less and less, until eventually, I was saying, 'I'm in the ... I want my ... are you ...?' and the less I said, the more powerfully the girls reacted. A number of girls even hugged each other and turned their back on me as I told (as if that would save them - Mmmwahahahahaha).

It's simple - the more I left out, the more they filled in. This is the fear of empty spaces at work. As people, we don't like incomplete thoughts, we don't like unfinished ... we don't ... Presented with a vacuum the mind rushes to fill it. If you are creating images of beauty, of joy, then your listeners will, of their own accord, fill any gaps you leave with whatever is most beautiful to them, most joyful. If you are telling them a scary story (and we will discuss the pros and cons and some guidelines for the telling of scary stories to children later, in the section entitled 'Scaring Them Silly, Because They Want You To' on page 65) and you leave images, thoughts, phrases incomplete, your listeners will fill that vacuum with whatever is most scary to them. You have to be careful, as with Language of Comment, because if you have left too much too blank it won't work, but done right it can be very powerful. As with most things, it's a matter of balance; do it too much and too obviously and you'll start to annoy your listeners. The best approach is to *really listen* to your audience as they listen to you, and make a judgement. The more you do that listening the better you get at it.[11]

There is one very powerful way in which you can supplement your use of the Fear of Empty Spaces and this is by using not words, but gestures. This opens up a whole new area in your development as a storyteller – what do you do with your body when you're telling a story?

☞ Characterisation

There are many things you can do physically to make your story more vivid in the mind of your listener or listeners, to make the characters inside your story more 'real' until they practically jump out as themselves. Of the available methods, let's start with using your voice.

Characterisation I – Voice

Your voice is part of your body and just like any other part of your body it can be trained and developed. It's not my aim in this book to teach you how to make your voice strong enough to talk to a packed hall. What you're doing is going to be much more intimate. But your voice is important.

Years ago, I was on a long train journey. I was on my way home after a few days away storytelling. I was tired. The train was crowded and, yes, it was delayed. Further up the carriage, I heard a young girl speak: 'Mummy, tell me "Goldilocks and the Three Bears" again!'

Then some grown up speech I couldn't hear, and, 'No, Mummy, tell it to me again!'

Then I heard a very tired mother begin (for the I don't know how manyeth time!) that story. Mum sounded very tired, like she was going through the motions but still things went OK until she reached the point where Daddy Bear expresses mystification that some unknown person seems to have usurped his privileged seating facility, but mother was exhausted and uncomfortable and so the words, 'Somebody has been sitting in my chair' were delivered in a tired mother sort of voice. Her child could not let that pass: 'Mummy,' she protested, 'that doesn't even *sound* like a bear!'

Her tone was all astonishment and outrage, and she got me thinking. This child was only 3 or 4 years old. My guess is she had never heard a real bear speak (I haven't, and I'm much older than her). Nonetheless, she had strong views on what a bear in a story should sound like.

Ultimately, in a story, we expect a bear's voice to be bear shaped. It needs to be big. We think of bears as being slow moving (they aren't, but let that pass) and so we expect a bear's voice also to move slowly. Now, of course, you already know this and you can already do this, but I am going to give you some tips for creating character voices that will fit your characters and will mean that, once your listener has heard them, you can return to them accurately (you already know who will correct you if you don't!). This means that when you want to, you can get rid of phases like 'said the bear' or 'the bear answered' because they aren't needed. This means taking you, the storyteller, further out of the picture. The picture builds, uninterrupted, in your listener's imagination. Your child's imagination itself builds and they draw closer to your story.

So, why don't we start this task by creating a bear voice? In your mind, imagine your bear. Here are some questions to help you:

He-bear or she-bear?
How old?
Strong? Or weak?
How big?
What colour?
Happy? Or sad?
Does it have family? Friends?
Where is it?
When was/is this?
Is it on all fours? Standing? Lying down?
What is it doing?
What is or has been done to it?

Have you got a clear image of that bear? Good. Now, *be* that bear. Feel yourself as that bear. Now say something as that bear.

What happened? How did you sound? Great!

Now, track back in your mind. You can do this reflectively and I want you to try and do this without 'becoming' the bear again. Just track back in your mind to what you just did and answer the following questions:

What did your face do?
What did your mouth do?
What did your head do?
What did your eyes do and where did they look?
What did your shoulders do?
What did your arms and hands do?

Done? Great. Now be the bear again.

So, were you able to just go straight back into your bear voice? Fantastic! So now we're going to get more specific and explore how what you do with your face can change your voice and change the characters you create in your storytelling.

Characterisation II – Facial Expressions

I have no idea how many languages there are in the world,[12] but I do know what happens when I have to talk with someone and I can't speak their language and they can't speak mine. We both start pulling faces and making gestures. Even without words we still have the ability to communicate, and this is what the next part of this book is about.

When we have no shared language we default to the things we all start with, the language of what we can indicate with gestures, such as 'that', 'this', 'big' or 'small', 'heavy', 'light', 'fast', 'slow', 'outside of', 'inside of', 'through', 'on top of'. And we also indicate how we feel about these things.

How do we indicate how we feel when we have no words to evoke it? Simple – we pull faces. It is believed that there are six facial expressions that are the same across all humanity. Whatever languages we speak, whatever culture we come from, we show these six emotions on our faces in the same way.

They are:

Happiness:

Sadness:

Anger:

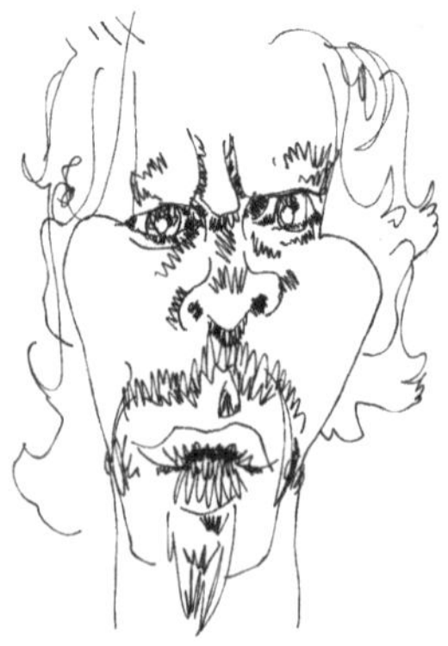

Fear:

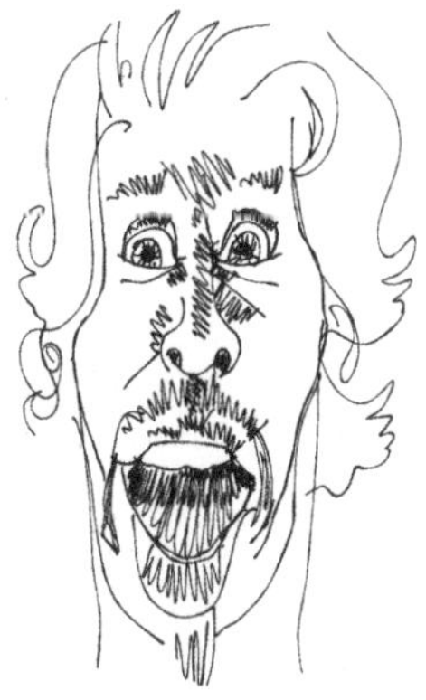

Surprise:

Disgust:

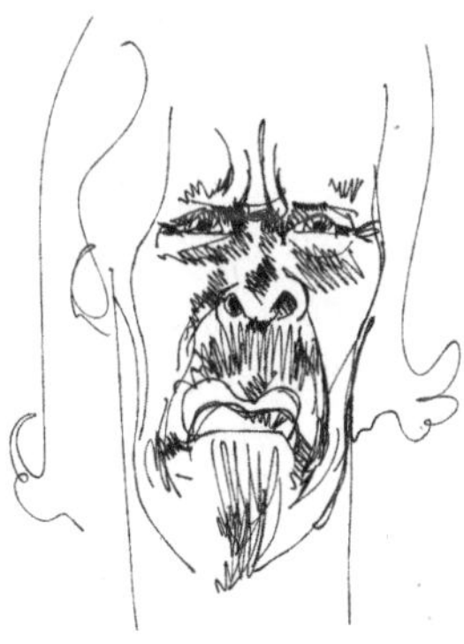

Take a minute now to pull each of these faces in turn, holding each face for five seconds. Did you notice that, as you pulled the faces, you felt your emotions change a little too? Now, whatever it was your bear just said, can you go back to it and, without changing the words, say it again as:

Happy Bear
Sad Bear
Angry Bear
Scared Bear
Surprised Bear
Disgusted Bear

How did your character voice sound? Did you feel it while you were 'being' the character? Isn't it wonderful just how easy it is? Now, go back to the Quest story you created earlier; I have a challenge for you.

Find two characters in your story and something they can say to one another. Got it? Good. How does Character 1 look, feel, speak? How does Character 2 look, feel, speak? Got that? Now ...

1. Tell, as yourself, the part of the story that leads up to this exchange between characters.
2. Then be your first character and speak as them.
3. Immediately shift into being your second character, and have them answer.
4. Shift back into yourself, the storyteller, and take the story on.

How did that feel? Sound? Look? Now, tell your whole story from start to finish, *being very conscious of deliberately shifting from storyteller to character, from character to character* until you reach the end.

My guess is that your story is coming on a lot.

Characterisation III - Body, Head and Eyes

As previously mentioned, when somebody listens to a story, research shows that they actually create their own mental simulation of the story inspired by what they see and hear the storyteller do and say. I *know* I've said this before but this is very important.

I first got a glimpse of how powerful this is when watching a storyteller/musician called Nick Hennessey perform. His story featured two smiths, one iron, one silver, competing to impress an emperor. At one point, Hennessey described the silversmith making a fish entirely of silver. The smith showed it to the emperor, carried it to a fountain's pool, lowered it into the water and let it go. The silver fish came to life and swam away.

Now, that's just words but, while in the audience, I *saw* what he described. Very skilfully, Hennessey worked with my attention and enhanced it. So, he:

- Talked *about* the silversmith as himself, Nick Hennessey, talking to a roomful of listeners in a room above a pub.
- Became the silversmith talking *to* the emperor. As such, he broke eye contact with us. Why? Because the silversmith can't see us. He's in the story and we're not.
- He, as storyteller, with eyes on us, told us that the smith took the fish to the pool.
- He, as the silversmith, cupped his hands as if carrying a silver fish. His eyes were on the 'fish' in his hands. He walked carefully towards a 'pool', bent his legs and back, lowered his hands and then, as he opened his hands, had his eyes follow a path as if following the movement of a fish that had just swum quickly from his hands.
- As storyteller, he told us it swam away. This was just confirmation - we'd already *seen* it!

I have another example, from a storyteller called Phil McDermott. Phil is a genius at creating visual effects with no special effects budget at all. He was telling me a story of a clever peasant girl whose wit was being tested by an arrogant, young, rich man. He challenged her to bring him a gift hat was not a gift. Phil said, 'So, she thought and thought, and then, three days later, she brought to him ...'

He stopped talking altogether and began walking towards me, his hands cupped as if holding something. As he approached, he was making the purring, cooing sound that doves make. He made as if to give me the dove, opened his hands and suddenly his gaze shot upwards as the sound he made abruptly became the sound of, first, an explosion of doves' wings and then, as his eyes arced up and rightwards, the sound of wingbeats receding. To me, it was a moment of pure magic. I saw the bird that was not right in front of my eyes.

Now, in your mind, track back. Do you remember the exercise we did when you told as you, then Character 1, then Character 2? Was anyone there with you? If so, you can ask them. If not, you will have to ask yourself (but ask honestly!). When you moved from character to character did your body change? Did the direction of your eyes alter?

It should do. If one character is talking to another, surely they will look at each other? So, if you show your audience two people talking to each other but looking in the same direction, your audience will be imagining them on a bus or somehow sat side by side. Great if that's what you mean, but not if it isn't.

We've all fallen foul of this! I was once telling a story in which a character was holding a baby. I was so casual about my shift from character holding baby to storyteller holding nothing that, effectively, my whole audience saw me drop a baby on the floor. It was commented on afterwards.

So, how do we work on this aspect of our storytelling? Let's start with head and eyes.

Go back to that little scene in your story where two characters reacted to each other. If you have a listener with you, great. If you don't, choose something in the room to be your point of focus or choose an area of your room where your 'audience' is. Look at them and tell the 'storyteller to audience' part of your story.

Stop.

Shift into Character 1. Where are they looking? Is the character to whom they are speaking taller than them or shorter? Still or moving? When this is clear, *be* the character and look and speak accordingly.

Stop.

Turn your body to face the other way. Become Character 2. Which way are they looking? Clue – if Character 1 was taller and looked downwards then Character 2 must look upwards (I've seen this go wrong and it's hilarious! As dialogue advances characters seem to grow unendingly and hobbits become basketball players). Have Character 2 speak. If the conversation between the characters continues, carry on, shifting as you need, until you return to being the storyteller, looking at your listeners.

How did it go? It's kind of obvious, but it doesn't necessarily feel easy. Nothing feels easy the first time you do it, but you can only improve on something once you've done it once, as Graham Langley once said ...

 Gesture

Now, is there a part of your story when a character does something? When you are leading an audience through a story you are essentially leading them blind. They follow you with absolutely no idea where they are going, but they are trusting you to lead them.

Gesture and Action is another area where you can accidentally make your audience stumble. Do this too often and they will cease to trust you as a guide.

For example, do you remember when I told you how Nick Hennessey, as the silversmith, released an invisible fish into an invisible pool that, thanks to the skill and precision of his movements, was 'visible' to me? Well, when the fish had swum away, he very cleverly stepped back from the edge of the pool before he continued his story. This allowed it to discreetly fade from our attention. If he'd stepped forward, he would have stepped into the pool. So, because you don't want to get wet feet either, don't make your trusting audience stumble as they follow your lead.

We shall now start exploring what you can do with your whole body. You use your body and your hands all the time to support your expressiveness, it's natural. To get better at it you will now have to do some things that are deliberately unnatural, artificial, because it is the best way to make you consciously aware of how you use your body to support your speech.

Years ago, I was working every week as storyteller in a number of hospitals. One day a teacher led me to the first of two isolation cubicles where two very poorly young people (brother and sister) were recovering from bone marrow transplants. They both had the same kind of cancer. They had no immune system and hence their isolation, even from each other. As we approached I was told of their situation, their ages and their names. I started thinking of stories I might want to tell, based on age and gender, leaving the final decision until I met them. At the door, the teacher said to me, 'Oh, by the way, they neither of them speak any English.'

And then I was through the door and had to do something. So, for the first patient, the teenage girl, I told the story of the 'Three Billy Goats Gruff' without any speech at all, but only using movement, gestures and sound effects. It worked! So I did the same for her brother and it also worked. They smiled, they fixated (i.e., their attention was fixated on the story) and they laughed at the funny bits, looked worried at the dangerous bits. This made me think of an experiment. Back in the classroom, where other child patients were assembled, I told them what had just happened and that I would now tell the same story to them, also without speech. My challenge to them? Once they'd figured out what the story was, they were to add the words to what I was doing and tell the story to my actions. It worked. So, your body alone can tell a story. It's how the English get by on holiday.

Still using the Quest story that you created earlier, I want you to find a mirror, full length if possible but half length minimum. Stand in front of the mirror and prepare to tell your story.

But you are *not allowed to speak*.

I want you to tell the story completely silently, only using gestures, facial expressions, head movement, sight line change and body and hand movement. This can be done!

How did that feel? How did you do? Were you clearly able, as you looked at your reflection, to separate narrator from character? Did you finish the character action before returning to being narrator? Or did you drop the baby? Not sure? Let's do it again, but this time, the narrator is allowed to speak.

So, tell the story in front of a mirror. When you come to the character, think their dialogue, mime it, but don't speak it.

Was that easier? Clearer? Good. You are on the brink of mastering something really powerful, a technique you can use to really make images burst inside your listeners' minds.

Word Substitution

Now, telling your whole story, or all of the characters' parts, without using speech is a little unusual, a little artificial. Good. That made you pay attention to what you were doing, and it was interesting, wasn't it? So now we are going to get the best of both speech and silence.

Can you think of a part of your story when you, as storyteller, have described your character doing something, performing an action? This will not be one of the sections when you have 'become' the character, but simply when you, as storyteller, have told us what they were doing. Got one? Good.

Now you are going to tell that section of the story to the mirror. Do this now, so you are clear about how this section of the story goes.

And are you clear at what point you are describing the character doing something? Good - now I want you to tell the section again and, just as you get to the point where you would describe the character doing something, stop talking, become the character and *show us the character doing it.* Then shift back into being narrator and take the story on.

So what happened? Did it work? When you get very deft at this you can slip very quickly from Description to Action, from narrator to character and back, and it is very powerful. I remember I did a gig once and a friend of mine, who hasn't seen me work often, was talking to me afterwards in great excitement saying it was amazing because he'd seen things in my hands that weren't in my hands. That was when I substituted the words with an action.

Have a think through your story and see how many places there are where a) you can do this and b) where it will help the story if you do. Got some? Good. Do it. And, while you're doing it, take a moment to observe what happens if you do too much? This is a matter of judgement but it's important. When I work with young children I have to be very insistent that they are storytelling, not acting. Because if they can tell me that two knights fought hard, their swords flashing in the sun, we *see* that far more vividly than when we are presented with the spectacle of two kids running around waving their empty hands at one another. At no point should you allow your storytelling to become bad mime.

Place – Why Baddies are Always Right

Now that you are using Voice, Gesture and Movement to make the characters in your stories more real, we need to think a little more about the world in which they exist. As in, where they are in relation to their surroundings and each other? We've already looked at how they look at each other in relation to both position and posture/stature. Let's look now at where they are.

In 2023 I was commissioned by the International Shakespeare Festival held at Theatr Globe in Neuss, Germany. They asked me to perform a monologue based on a Shakespeare play so I chose *Macbeth*. I had no props, no sound effects, sound, nor lighting. The previous year I had performed simply sitting in a chair in the middle of the stage as I told *Shakespeare's Back Stories*, the folktales that narratively underpin some of Shakespeare's best-known plays. It worked. I vanished and the stories appeared but I felt that, for *Macbeth*, something more was needed.

So I used posture, gesture and voice as we have already explored it to create quick and distinguishable characterisations for Macbeth, Lady Macbeth, Duncan, MacDuff and Lady MacDuff. But I needed also to evoke the circumstances in which they existed and interacted.

Here I had an advantage not always available to storytellers – I knew beforehand the space in which I was to perform. Theatr Globe has a large, raised stage facing rows of seats that curve semicircularly around the stage (a bit, not too much nor too close at the sides) and two gallery levels above. The front of the stage is a ramp that drops 3 or 4ft to ground level where the audience sits. I could picture the space so, as well as posture/stature/movement and voices of characters, I could think about where things would happen in space.

As I devised/rehearsed, I began to place and fix locations. Dunsinane Castle, Macbeth's home and where much of the villainy takes place, would always be upstage right (right in the audience's perception, but to the left in mine). Lady Macbeth, in her dream scene, would enter, from the audience's perspective, from the right. Of course, she didn't really enter from anywhere but I, as narrator, moved to my left-hand side, then turned to my right as I became Lady Macbeth. Without boring you with all my cues and blocking, I place 'baddies' to the right of the audience's perception, 'goodies' to the left. Why?

According to American communication consultant Jerry Weissman, it's a matter of our perceptive psychology. In his book, *Presenting to Win*, Weissman argues that, because of our writing system and the way we read from left to right, we are conditioned to look up and left for beginnings. He says Hollywood knows this and places the entry of characters accordingly – 'goodies' to the left of screen and 'baddies' to the right. Presumably this only works for people who are native in cultures that use the Latin alphabet. Arabic reads right to left, also Hebrew and, traditionally, Japanese and Chinese scripts are read in columns, top to bottom. I don't know if people rooted in these systems have different perceptive systems psychologically. But I followed Weissman's argument in *Macbeth*, placing 'baddies' to the right and 'goodies' to the left. I do the same, more simply, when choosing eye lines for characters in other stories. 'Goodies' tend to look and speak from my right to the left, which places them on the left in the audience's perception. And 'baddies' are always to the right. Next time you're watching Netflix see if you can observe this in action.

A key thing to bear in mind is, as I mentioned earlier in relation to Nick Hennessey's creation of a pool, once you have 'placed' an object in the audience's mind, keep it there. If a king admires the bunch of flowers he has received, then places them on a table to his left and then, after a such a busy day, he takes off his heavy crown and rests it on a silk cushion to his right, when he rushes to put his crown back on because his rest is being disrupted, please remember where things are, or your audience will 'see' the king hurriedly place a bunch of flowers on his head!

But now, what if, in your storytelling, you have to become a servant who enters from the left and approaches the king. Where is the king now? If he's straight in front of the servant, is the crown between him and the servant or is it the flowers? If the servant has entered from the audience's left, it's between. If the servant has entered from the king's right then that's the audience's left and your servant has just lightly lifted up and smelt the crown. In words these things sound very complicated. In truth, they're not. Just imagine vividly, make some movement or, if it helps, draw some sketches. As always, with practise, you can learn to do this in the moment. Consistency of locations and placement is a key part of how much your audience will believe in the world of your story.

Give it a try. Walk, move, pace through your story. Have your characters interact with objects in location and practise returning to where they would be for specific characters.

So how was that? Is your story really flying now? I bet it is! Next, we are going to explore making your audience fly, or rather flee - except they won't. You are going to learn how to scare the hell out of them, and they will stay right where they are, because they are loving it! Weirdly, they'll even thank you afterwards.

Scaring Them Silly, Because They Want You To

Actually it's more about scaring them safely. One of the two drama therapists who devised the Six-Part Story Process, Mooli Lahad, also did some very interesting research into the value of scary stories. Working with young Israeli people who, as part of their national service, had been involved in military conflict, he selected two groups. All members of both groups had experienced the same or similarly traumatising events (inasmuch as anyone can be said to experience the same thing as another). He divided this large group into two groups. Group A were suffering badly from the effects of their experiences, Group B less so. Essentially, Group A were suffering Post-Traumatic Stress Disorder (what used to be called shell-shock) and Group B weren't. Lahad made a study of the stories these young people had been told as children. He discovered that the men in Group A, who were suffering PTSD, had not been told scary stories when they were little and those in Group B, who seemed to be coping with the horror of their experiences better, had been told scary stories when they were little. He concluded that exposure to scary stories when young had equipped Group B with the necessary psychological mechanisms and the ability to process fear. Those in Group A did not seem to have the same ability to process fear and they suffered much more from the similar experiences and emotions that Group B had felt but dealt with better.

Interesting, no? Very often, when I go to tell stories to children, a grown-up will say to me, 'Now, don't scare them!' Then I meet the children and ask them what sort of story they'd like to hear and, most of the time, most of the children will chorus, 'Scareeeee ...'. Hearing a scary story is a safe place for a child to explore a very challenging emotion, fear, and they seem to have an instinctive wish to make that exploration. Adults, it seems, fear to say what children need to hear.

Now, I'm not advising you to show your pre-school children *Driller Killer*. I'm very careful when telling scary stories to children, working always to sense the difference between a hush caused by rapt attention and one caused by misery. I don't see any value in traumatising children and so the scary stories I tell vary according to the age. They also vary in the telling as I listen to their responses. The older they get the more graphic the description gets. If they're young it stays at a safer level. Violence is present and children are told about it but, if they are young (under 6) I don't use language so vivid that it really puts them in it. There's no need.

Let me give you an example. There is a story I know as 'Orange, Lemon and Lime'.[13] In this story, a mother, who is perfectly kind to her youngest daughters, is always cruel to her eldest child, a boy. As part of this story, the mother cuts her son's throat and orders her daughters to get knives, cut off the flesh and bury the bones in the yard. Then she cooks pies made of her son and feeds them that night to her oblivious husband. Don't fall off your chair, but I do tell this story to 5-year-olds. In fact, I was on my way to a Hallowe'en party one year at which my wife and my mother-in-law were also to be guests. I had been asked to tell stories for about an hour. I told my mother-in-law the bones (excuse the pun) of this story and said that I would tell it. She was appalled, protested vigorously, saying I couldn't possibly tell this story to children. I did. On that occasion, the way I told the story was that the older child who gets killed is a girl (it's how I heard it first). Later in the evening, when all my storytelling was finished, a little boy, flanked by his mother, approached me because he wanted to tell me that he'd heard that story before and, though he liked my telling, when he had previously heard it the child who gets murdered was a boy. My mother-in-law heard him. He was 5 years old.

It has to be a balancing act. This story also features a song with a jaunty tune and exceptionally gruesome lyrics that describe what has happened to the boy/victim. I get the children to sing it with me as they follow the discorporate spirit as he flies about the town collecting gifts for his sisters, his father, and also an item for his mother that becomes the means of his revenge and of his rebirth, composed of dust and his mother's blood.

Now, without it being graphic, this is a very grisly story and children love it. I told it once to a group of more than forty children at an event in an outdoor museum in Yorkshire, attended by children from various local schools. After my half-hour session was over another group came in, then another, after which I had my lunch break. I left the small building where I was telling and began walking towards the museum cafe. As I approached the main path I heard a sound; a group of more than thirty children were already on the path, walking in step and singing at the tops of their youthful voices,

> My Mother she killed me and put me in pies!
> My Father he ate me and said it was nice!
> My two little sisters they picked at my bones
> And buried me under cold marble stones!

I was enormously moved and also grateful. I think the fact that the children sing the song with me (it gets repeated four times), meaning that, effectively, the children are telling the story with me, gives them a sense of being at least partly in control of the experience. This is not like a film in which you just open your eyes and your psyche to whatever the director has decided to put in you, is it?

In other instances, when telling scary stories, I've had children shriek, put their hands up in the air (just like they do in cartoons – I never knew that really happened!). I've seen whole classes, sat on the floor, flattening like a field of wheat when a helicopter is landing as I rise up and do my giant/monster voice, then sit up giggling, and more than once, a group of teenage girls has burst into spontaneous applause when the baddie gets his comeuppance at the end of a serial killer story called 'Mr Fox'.[14] Scary stories seem to be doing something for them.

So, what are my guidelines for telling scary stories to young people? Well, if it's your own kids you won't need my guidelines because you know your children, but if it isn't, you may find the following helpful:

- Age 5 and below: No shouting! Very young children, when they hear shouting, seem to think it must be that you're shouting at them and it upsets them. If a character in your story has to shout, 'cheat it out' and pretend to shout. So, you make the angry face, alter the tone of your voice, but keep the volume down.
- Age 5 and below: Though you can have real violence, real horror in a story, keep the audience a certain distance from it by not going into vivid description. So, in the story discussed above I might say, 'She took a knife and drew it across his neck' or I might say, 'She cut his throat from ear to ear' but I would **not** say, 'She cut and the knife dragged through his flesh. Blood hissed and spurted from the gaping wound as the room was filled with the stench of blood and with the desperate sound of his gurgling, choking death!' Allow the children to create age-appropriate images for themselves.
- All ages: The best technique of all for telling scary stories is to leave things out. We talked earlier about the fear of empty spaces, do you remember? So, you might say, 'She put the blade to his neck and ... the twins, outside, had heard their mother's raised voice and now they came running in, only to see ... and imagine their horror when their mother looked up at them, her eyes wild, and said ... (etc. etc.).' Does that make sense? It's very powerful, because your listener will fill the gaps according to their own prescription.
- All ages: Above all, don't be gratuitous. 'Orange, Lemon and Lime' fulfils a genuine psychological need, the need to explore the fear of maternal anger (albeit somewhat exaggerated). Teenage girls have thanked me for telling 'Mr Fox' 'because there are people like that out there', I never tell scary stories that dwell on horror and unpleasant sensations purely for their own sake. This is probably just a matter of personal taste.

At this stage, all this may not yet be relevant to you or the story you have already created, which may not be a scary story. However, the techniques for making a scary story scary can also be used to make an exciting story more exciting. Just heighten the risk, sharpen the danger. Later in the book we shall explore two Forms of Story that you can use to deliberately create a scary story and, when we get there, you will already know how to make the best of it. And there is a value to this. I have learned, during my years of storytelling, that if children get the chance to tell me a scary story it's quite likely to be one of the stories I heard from other children when I was their age.

Children's Independent Culture is a known, proved thing. And I have noticed, returning to storytelling with children after the long hiatus of the Covid lockdown, that I have to lower the maturity level of stories for children who passed significant parts of their childhood under lockdown. So kids who were aged 5 to 11 years old missed out on all that bouncing off other kids, hearing and telling things to and with other children that, though they might be factually inaccurate, would nonetheless have contributed to their emotional development. I have noticed similar things in some blind and visually impaired children. All the rough and tumble seems to actually be an important part of how we grow up and the telling of scary stories can be a healthy part of that rough and tumble. I noticed this most sharply after the pandemic, but a child psychologist I met told me that the pandemic accelerated something that was actually already happening. We live in an ever more screen-facing - not human-facing - automated world. We order food, clothing, tickets, without human interaction, we buy goods at self-checkout (if we go to a shop at all), meaning younger people are growing up without the level of social interaction previous generations learnt when buying goods, tickets and services face to face. The mental and emotional maturity of some young people is plummeting. Storymaking and storytelling, sitting face to face, working socially/collaboratively with young people, may, in some small measure, work to counteract this?

Proving the Pudding

So, you've created, shaped and sharpened your first story, a Quest, and you have spoken it out loud. Take a break. Perhaps leave it until tomorrow but, before you sleep, go through it again in your mind. If you do that, when you wake up the story will have moved from your working memory to your permanent memory.

Whether you leave it overnight or not, when you're ready and if you haven't already, tell your story to a member of its intended audience, i.e. your child or a child you have care of or contact with. Then reflect, track back in your mind: how did it go? Ask them, did they like it? What did they like about it? What can they remember of it (this one will amaze you)? They may remember more than you think. They may remember you saying things you don't remember saying. They may even remember things you *didn't* say but which they perceived vividly because of what you did say. You just gave them a gift, one they can keep for all their life, one they can share or give away a thousand times and yet still have.[15] You just gave them a story.

Memory III – Take it for a Walk

One more memory technique that many people find very effective is, when you're learning something, take it for a walk.

Think about it for a moment. At the time our earliest ancestors lived, they must have been walking pretty much from the moment they woke to the moment they slept. Before we were farmers or herders we were hunters and, to a much greater extent, foragers and gatherers, walking around a complex environment finding a variety of things to eat. So we needed to remember routes between sites of interest.

I lost about 80 per cent of my sight when I was 25 and one of the things I've noticed is how much I now struggle with my topographical memory. I am always remembering interesting things that someone has said to me but can't remember who they were or where I was when I heard it. When we moved home ten years ago, my wife learned her way around our new district in a matter of weeks. Six years later, I was still struggling to connect isolated locations into a coherent map of places and their relationship to one another.

You will, perhaps, already have noticed that this bears a relationship to how we remember the elements of a story or a story structure? Not just on their own but in terms of how they relate to each other. And how we can choose a route through a story just as we might through a locality.

Our ancestors will have done most of their thinking as they walked around their locality. Like them, we can still do great thinking at 3 miles per hour. If you choose a route that you know well enough that you can walk it almost automatically, it frees your mind up to do other things than pay attention to where you're going but, *because you are moving*, your mind is busy enough with direction, motion, balance, orientation, that it frees your imagination and concentration from all the endless chatter that might otherwise distract you. I can't prove it but I bet this is one of the ways people find value in making a pilgrimage? Walking allows you to absorb yourself in your thoughts.

When I'm working on a story that I have partially composed and that I need to practise, I put a pair of headphones in my ears and go for a walk. This means that if I need to talk out loud (and frequently I do) people just assume I'm having a conversation on my mobile phone[16] and ignore me.

So, you've created a Quest story. You've applied a series of different techniques in order to develop it and, because you've applied them to the same story, you've been able to observe what each technique does? Good – now take it for a walk and feel it deepen even more.

Further Proving of the Pudding – Example Stories

With a view to helping you on your journey to becoming a spellbinding storyteller, I shall be giving you some example stories, after you've met each story structure and *after* you have made your Memory Palace for each succeeding story structure. Each story is chosen to exemplify this or that story structure and I include them simply to show you how much can be done imaginatively from so small, but specific, a structure. In some cases I will give more than one example story and this is simply to show you how much variety can exist between different stories that, nonetheless, share the same basic structure at their core. These example stories are *not* intended for you to read to your children. If you're reading this book I have assumed you are an adult and I have written these stories with an adult reader in mind. You can, of course, share them with your kids if you think them age and otherwise appropriate. However, doing so will do nothing to improve you as a storyteller, and bear in mind it is you that your children most want to hear. It is your eye contact, lost to them as you read a book or screen, which is so important to them.

When you've finished the exercises in this book you can, of course, quickly learn the bones of these example stories. Your awareness of story structure will help you to do this. Then you can retell *your own version* of the example stories specific to you, the teller, and your exact audience. This is something I would positively encourage you to do because this is exactly how these amazing stories have survived long enough to come down to us. This is the essence of traditional storytelling.

Essentially, the example stories are written for you and I hope you enjoy them. As you read them you will notice that most, if not all of them, feature either love or death or both. And? What can you think of in your life that has ever had more elemental power and impact than your experiences of love and death? Better your children explore these huge themes within the safe bounds of a story first and through the gift of imagination than as raw and shocking experience, surely?

Example Story - 'Theseus and the Minotaur'

As this is your first example story, I will number the stages as we go so you can refer back to the story structure that is now lodged in your Memory Palace. Hopefully, this will show you just how much variety and inventiveness are assisted by a clear structure, and how limitation can inspire, rather than restrict creativity.

1

It was only a few months ago that Theseus had arrived in Athens, had made himself known to and had been acknowledged proudly by his father, King Aegeus. He had not yet grown used to his new life but the people of Athens had accepted him lovingly as their prince and all, including Theseus, were happy.

2

Then, as a certain month approached, Theseus noticed how people grew glum, even taciturn. He felt it. Suddenly no one was cracking jokes. No one was throwing parties. No one told him why. So he asked Aegeus: 'Father, why has the mood of the city and its people changed so much? Yours, too?'

King Aegeus winced, and sucked air between his teeth, then,

'The people are sad, and I am sad, because the time of the Tribute is coming.'

Theseus was stunned. What tribute? To whom was it paid?

Aegeus explained that Minos, the great and powerful King of Crete, whose ships commanded all the seas around Hellas, exacted a tribute from different city states all over Hellas. Athens, in common with other states, was obliged to send, every year, nine youths and nine maidens to Crete. Theseus asked why.

'Because,' said Aegeus, 'there is a monster hidden inside a great maze, the Labyrinth. The monster has, they say, the body of a man and the head of a bull. Each state must send these eighteen young people, who then must walk into the Labyrinth. None come out.'

'Why?' demanded Theseus.

'Because the Minotaur eats them,' said Aegeus, 'They keep the Minotaur imprisoned in that maze and send him victims so that his hunger never drives him out. It is all to hide their shame!'

'Shame?'

'Yes, shame. Minos has a wife, Queen Pasiphae, who gave birth to that monster.'

'Why don't they kill it?' demanded Theseus.

'It is the queen's child!'

'I don't understand,' said Theseus, 'child or not, it is a monster and should be killed.'

'Monster or not,' answered his father, 'it is her child and must be spared. When you have children yourself, you will understand. Until that time, you won't'.

'How then are the victims chosen?' asked Theseus, but Aegeus changed the subject. It was some days later, and from other people, that Theseus learned that the victims were chosen by lot. All the names of young women and men of the right age were put in a bowl and the priest would draw names out. So it was that they were chosen. Theseus realised he himself was of the right age.

So, next he asked his father if his own name could be drawn by lot and Aegeus answered, 'Absolutely not! You are exempt and your name cannot be chosen!'

Theseus wanted to know why not.

'Because,' Aegeus spluttered, 'you mustn't be! You are, one day, to be the king of the people.'

'Father,' said Theseus, 'surely, if I am to be king of the people, then I must be *of* the people? Put my name in with theirs.'

Aegeus was reluctant but Theseus insisted. When, a fortnight later, the ships came from Crete and the lots were drawn, Theseus was among those selected.

3

He boarded the ship with eight other young men and nine young women. No one spoke. Arriving at Crete, they were ordered off and driven on like slaves. They were slaves. Arriving at King Minos' great capital, Knossos, Theseus was the only one who seemed able to be amazed by it. The others just looked at the ground and didn't so much walk as shamble, their every step another step closer to their death. But Knossos was magnificent and Theseus' eyes went everywhere!

The new sacrifices were lined up so the king could inspect them. Minos looked, as he had done for so many years, down a line of miserable victims. There were many more than the eighteen from Athens because tribute was also paid by Corinth, by Sparta, by Megara and Eubeoa, by Thebes, by Marathon, and all the many islands of the Sporades and Cyclades. He looked down on them all from the great height of his royal throne.

4

Next to him sat his daughter, Ariadne. Princess Ariadne also looked down at this year's line of victims and saw, as she had seen before, a long line of youths and maidens of the same age as herself and yet of how different a demeanour! She was a royal. Her arms were braceleted in gold. Theirs hung with iron chains. She was a priestess, adorned with cosmetics chosen specifically to align her to the Cosmos, so her neck, her wrists, were ornamented with bright crystals. Her face was painted with beautiful make-up, her eyelashes with antimony. Their faces were decorated with grime and bruises. But there was one who stood out as her eyes scanned the ranks. He stood with his head held high. She saw the intelligence in his curious eyes. She saw the way his eyes darted and enquired, taking in every detail of the great hall, as if intent on learning everything he could about it. Then she saw those quick and dancing eyes spot her and they stopped their dance. He gazed at her. She held his gaze. This youth did not look, to Ariadne, like a slave. He looked like a leader.

Ariadne made enquiries later that day. That youth? He was one of the Athenians. She had servants investigate this Athenian for her and she learned, to her astonishment, that he was the son of King Aegeus. That he had, himself, demanded his name be put into the bowl, that he should face the same selection, the same danger, as any one of his people. She wondered, would her father do this? Would she do this? She longed to know him better and so, in disguise, she visited the quarters of the tribute slaves, moved among them until she found Theseus.

'Why are you here?' she asked.

'Because my name was selected.'

'How is it that your name could be selected?'

'Because I wished it so.'

'Do you not fear the Minotaur?'

'Not today – he isn't here! Today, I fear more to see disapproval in your lovely eyes.'

It was Ariadne who fled then. But she returned. She returned again and again to talk with Theseus. Whenever he asked her about herself she was evasive. He said to her that he could see she was of a noble family, which she admitted, blushing.

'I would say, in fact,' said Theseus, 'that you should be, might actually be, some kind of a priestess, or a princess, or both, or ...'

She fled again. But she came back, and back, until one day when she told him everything; she was daughter of King Minos, she was a princess and a priestess. It didn't really surprise her that this didn't surprise him.

'Good,' said Theseus, 'and now that we have grown so honest with one another, I can share honestly with you that you are beautiful and I should like to see you without disguise, without make-up, jewellery, titles, rank and robes. That is how I should like to see you.'

Ariadne blushed, in part with anger.

'You should not speak to me like that! You are a slave, brought here as tribute!'

'I am a king's son,' said Theseus, 'and I have come here of my own choosing, not as tribute to your father but as a sacrifice for my people. And anyway,' he continued, 'today, I can be as honest as I like, because tomorrow I shall be dead.'

Ariadne could not breathe, could not speak, so her eyes asked the question. She knew, as she asked, that it was not really a question.

'Yes,' said Theseus, 'my name has been chosen and tomorrow I am to be sent into the Labyrinth to meet the Minotaur.'

'But you seem so calm!' Ariadne gasped.

'If it is my destiny to become a king,' said Theseus, 'then I shall somehow kill the Minotaur, and if it is not, then no one shall hear me die.'

Ariadne had to leave – she couldn't bear it.

That night, as Theseus slept among the other young people, a hooded figure crept into the dormitory. They crept to where Theseus lay and gently woke him.

They pressed into his startled hands a large ball of twine and, next, the hilt of a short sword. The figure rose to leave but Theseus grabbed them by the wrist. 'This sword is short!' he hissed. 'What use is a short sword against a monster?'

'More use than a long sword!' said a voice, her voice. 'The tunnels in there are too narrow to swing a long sword!'

'And what's the twine for?' he asked,

'So you can find your way back out, if you live,' she answered.

Before she could pull herself away, Theseus pulled her hand towards him and kissed it. Then she was gone.

5

The next morning Theseus was ready. The short sword was hidden under the light cloak he wore. His hand kept the secret of the twine. The guards led him to the black mouth of the Labyrinth. Behind him, King Minos and Ariadne watched. A priestess was leading a prayer; when it was Ariadne's turn to lead the prayer Theseus heard her voice shake. Then, he entered the Labyrinth.

Reaching the first corner, he found, in the growing darkness, a dead tree root. Stooping, he tied the twine around the root. He bared the sword and, with the sword in his stronger hand and the twine in his other, he walked on. He tried to remember which way he'd turned so that he might reverse it later (if there was a later) but there were so many dizzying twists and turns that soon he knew it was useless and he would have to rely on the twine. Further and deeper he walked into that maze, which the genius inventor Daedalus had designed, darker and darker his path. After some time, he could see nothing. There was darkness pressing on his eyes, darkness squeezing his head. He could hear nothing but the sound of his feet scraping and crunching on the gritty floor, and the loud rasp of his own breath. He stopped. That wasn't his breathing.

All at once, the darkness rushed at him.

Inside that all-surrounding blackness, he sensed a greater darkness rushing at him. He felt the pounding of huge footsteps, heard the deep grunting of a beast. Instinctively, as he almost felt the density of that rush hit him, he threw himself on his back, stabbing upwards. It worked! Those tunnels reverberated with a massive, deafening bellow, a roar. He felt the hilt of the sword jerk in his hand as the Minotaur stumbled over him, forcing his sword's blade deeper into its body, but where? Its leg? Its groin? Abruptly, the weight on the sword lessened; the Minotaur had un-impaled itself. Theseus' hand, his body, was sticky with hot blood. Not his.

Now Theseus followed it. Following the sound of its movement (and he must have hit its leg, because now he could hear it was dragging one foot), Theseus came to a large circular hall inside the Labyrinth. Here there was some light,

though Theseus had neither time nor interest to work out where it came from. But now he could see his enemy.

The Minotaur had the body of a powerfully built man. Its thighs were immense, muscle lapping over muscle in great and bulging strength. Its midriff was thick, muscular, its chest massive, shoulders bunched, its arms were each like vast pythons. And its head was the heavy head of a bull, chestnut brown its fur, ferocious its eyes, eyes set in a heavy forehead, forehead topped with thick horns, horns tapering to sharp points, points that now were lowered, lowered to charge at Theseus. With an ear-splitting roar, the Minotaur attacked!

6

But Theseus was a wrestler, indeed, some say Theseus had invented the science of wrestling. He saw at once the Minotaur was over-balanced to the left as the wound that he had inflicted on his right leg was bleeding freely. So Theseus attacked by feinting first left, then dodging to the right. The Minotaur was over-balanced, over-committed and as he missed the agile youth, Theseus slashed (Ariadne was right! He could never have made that cut in here with a long sword) and opened a great wound down the Minotaur's neck and back. The Minotaur screamed, then hit the wall at the other side of the chamber. Opposite him, Theseus balanced his sword, shifted his feet so his right foot, foremost, pointed forwards as his sword did. His left foot, rearmost, pointed laterally. Theseus waited. The Minotaur, its breath coming now in agonised gasps, summoned up all its rage, all its indignation, and drove itself to its feet. Theseus could see that, thanks to his last cut, it now struggled to hold its head up. So it lowered its head and once more, it charged.

Theseus simply stood his ground, stiffened his wrist. The Minotaur ran, with its full weight, straight on to the point of Theseus's sword. The weight of it, the strength of it, drove the young man back, his back foot skidding, sliding. He felt the wall crash into him from behind as the full force of the Minotaur crushed into him from the front. He felt the force of it, smelt the stench of it, was smothered by the heat and fur of it, and then its weight sagged. It slid to his feet. It was dead! He had killed it!

He stared at it, his lungs heaving like bellows, his heart pounding like a large drum. He had killed the Minotaur!

Of course, he had long since dropped his ball of twine. Picking himself free of that heavy body he went looking, looking, until he found it. Winding it up as he went, he began to pick his way out of the Labyrinth, until at last he stepped out of that dark maze and into the sparkling palace of King Minos.

People gasped when they saw him, people rushed to question him. Some were thrilled, and some were frightened. Ariadne's eyes were shining. He had killed the Minotaur - what would he do next?

Ah, that is another story!

Memory IV – Cleaning the Palace

Before we go on, you need to do a bit of housework - sorry. Your Memory Palace needs cleaning. If you've used your Memory Palace correctly and have had some sleep since you first created it you should find that it is no longer necessary to use the images in it to retrieve the words that make each stage of the Quest. By now, the memory has been distributed in your brain. Take a moment to check, so, what are the stages of the Quest?

Got them? Good. Now you need to reimagine the Palace with no objects in it and get ready to make some new ones that will help you memorise the next story structure. Please read on.

Meet the Forms of Story

It is now time for you to meet the next of the Forms of Story. I shall try to present these Forms in such a way that, as your confidence grows, so too does the complexity of the Forms you will meet. I leave you to judge what level of complexity the child or children you are creating stories for are ready to hear. The next Form of Story I'd like us to play with is one called 'Journey and Return'.

2

Journey and Return

I'm sure you will start thinking of examples of this story structure as soon as I begin to sketch it out. Journey and Return is particularly popular in children's fiction. Journey and Return can be very similar to the Quest. After all, doesn't the protagonist of a Quest usually go on a journey? And usually come back? Think of the subtitle of *The Hobbit*, which is definitely a Quest: *The Hobbit, or There and Back Again*. The difference is to be found in the reason the journey starts in the first place. In the Quest, the protagonist *chooses* to begin their adventure. In Journey and Return, the protagonist is unwittingly flung into another world and an adventure that takes them far from home and, in addition to the adventures they have in whatever world they find themselves in, part of what drives the story is their need to get back home.

Think, for example, of *The Lion, the Witch and the Wardrobe*. The children don't mean to go to Narnia, they simply intend to explore the house where they find themselves. Think of the adventures of Sinbad the Sailor. Sinbad does mean to go on a gentle trading journey, but does not mean to be blown off course, nor sink, nor mistake a whale for an island, etc., etc. Who would? Lemuel Gulliver doesn't set out deliberately to travel to the world of the Lilliputians, nor does Mark Twain's Connecticut Yankee mean to travel in time and space to England at the time of King Arthur. It happens quite by accident when his factory foreman hits him on the head. Now contrast that with Bilbo Baggins, or Frodo Baggins, or any other rash, young and un-Hobbit-like Hobbit who features in *The Lord of the Rings*, or Luke Skywalker in *Star Wars*. They may not have leapt at the opportunity to go on an adventure, indeed, they are often reluctant and pass through intense periods of inner conflict before they decide, but in the end they do decide for themselves to go off on an adventure. Crucially, in Journey and Return, the journey starts without intent, by accident. Think of Dorothy and that hurricane.

There are numerous Hollywood films in this genre, of people who get accidentally shrunk and pilot their way around another characters' blood vessels, people who just get shrunk and journey into a world of being small, and so on. The character starts their journey accidentally, after which they can either struggle wholeheartedly to get home or they can, like the children in *The Lion, the Witch and the Wardrobe*, become completely involved in their new life, growing up, even ruling as monarchs until, abruptly, they lose all their royal pomp and possessions, lose their adulthood and find themselves, equally accidentally, stuck again in comparatively powerless, small bodies, and crammed together within the confines of a wardrobe that smells strongly of mothballs. Yuck.

Except, and here's a very clever twist by C.S. Lewis, they learn that one day, they will return to being kings and queens in Narnia, and it will turn out that Narnia is their real home and this life that they appear to have Returned to, with bad weather and schoolwork, later with gas bills, mortgages, sicknesses, disappointments and frustrations, is the foreign country from which they will one day return, the dream from which they will one day awaken. C.S. Lewis is in fact metaphorically telling quite another story, the Christian story.

There are many Journey and Return stories in the Irish tradition, in which protagonists accidentally step through the veil that divides our world from the world of the *sidhe*, or fairy. They live a whole life in the fairy world only to accidentally return again to find that very little time has passed in this world. Sometimes they change gender. Sometimes they journey accidentally into another world, spend a short time there and return only to find that in their absence decades or even centuries have passed.

Does this remind you of a classic of children's literature, *Where the Wild Things Are* by Maurice Sendak? Where Max goes to bed angry and frustrated, is transported to the world of the Wild Things, joins them in their wild rumpus and then returns home safely to his bed to sleep. His supper is by his bedside, still hot. Or *In the Night Kitchen*, also by Sendak? Mickey goes to bed but is disturbed by strange noises, witnesses the world around him transforming, is transported to a world where three enormous chefs bake a huge cake, where he flies an aeroplane made of cake dough and has further adventures until the miraculous world begins to fall away from him and he falls back safely into his bed. Both of these stories have been immensely successful, and small wonder; they are beautifully written and beautifully illustrated. But before all of that, they are beautifully imagined and beautifully constructed. They are constructed in very close conformity to the classic Form of Journey and Return.[17]

This particular Form is perhaps a very reassuring one for children. Children don't have much active choice in much of their lives. They are told to come to supper. They are told to go to bed. They are told to get in the car because, they are told, they are going to Granny's. For lucky children, these movements from one world to another are seldom alarming and end with a safe and happy homecoming but for some they are alarming and there is no happy homecoming. They are told they will be leaving this home. They are told that Mummy and Daddy are going to stop living together, and they are told they will spend three days with one and four with the other. They are told they are going to hospital, and Mummy and Daddy will only be able to be with them at certain times.

Active self-determination doesn't come until much later and so a story in which the protagonist is catapulted passively into a changed world will make immediate sense to them. In a way, it happens to them all the time. But with this Form there is always the comfort of a safe homecoming to a world that is still familiar, indeed, has not changed at all, no matter how wild, how alarming the adventure. That is, of course, if you *choose* to make the adventure wild and alarming; you may just as easily make the adventure endlessly indulgent or hilariously funny. I have worked with children who have created stories in which the protagonist is transported to a world made entirely of chocolate[18] or a world made entirely of poo.[19] For the children you are creating stories for you can make another, but important, variation. As an example, let me tell you about 'The Wanderings of Oisin'.

When I was about 14, Frank Delaney hosted a series on BBC television called *The Celts*. I was obsessed with this subject, this ancient culture, and absorbed every episode of this six-part series.[20] In one of these episodes, Delaney gave a brief summary telling of an Irish story he called 'The Wanderings of Oisin'. Even in such brief form (i.e. reduced to its bones, as we covered earlier) the story gripped me, moved me. I bought the book of the series, which contained long, written versions of four great Irish tales, but not that one. Years later, when I came across a reference to Oisin and his wanderings in a poem by W.B. Yeats, I dived into the study of Yeats, trying to find a version of that story. I found Yeats' poem, thick, heavy, comparatively ponderous, which, nonetheless, I grew to love, but that wasn't what I was looking for. The poetry is beautiful and, when I read it, I'm acutely conscious of the skill of the poet, of his language, his rhyming, his versification. I wanted *not* to be aware of that – I needed, as when I heard that brief version from Delaney, the walls to disappear, the storyteller themselves to disappear as I was transported into another world, a wild adventure, before being returned safely home again at the end of the story.

You see? That's the wonderful thing about Journey and Return as a Form. It is a story, it is any number of stories that can be about anything, and yet it is always also about story itself. It not only is a story, it represents story, which continually takes you from your familiar surroundings to quite another world in which strange things happen and then it brings you safely back again. Any child you tell a Journey and Return story to knows this instinctively.

But what was it about this particular story that moved me so, and what made it different to other Journey and Return stories? Eventually, I heard the story again, told by Joan Barr in a small room above that pub in West Yorkshire,[21] and I drank it in. Do you recall I told you that Quest stories feature a character choosing actively to go off on an adventure that they know may be dangerous? And that Journey and Return stories feature a character moving passively into another world, and after adventures they are returned safely home? 'The Wanderings of Oisin' is subtly different. In this story, the great warrior Fionn mac Cumhaill and his warriors, the Fianna, are camped by the shores of a lake ...

Example Story – 'The Wanderings of Oisin'

Among them is Oisin, Fionn's only son. On the far side of the lake, a beautiful woman appears, mounted on a horse. The warriors admire her from across the lake, wishing she would come closer. She does; she rides her horse directly over the still surface of the lake. As you may imagine, this puts the warriors in somewhat of an uproar and her once-desired approach is now terrifying them.[22] Fionn goes to greet her first and learns that she has come for that which he holds most dear in all the world, his son. Oisin is called over. The lady, Niamh, asks him if he would like to come away with her and live in love and joy with her forever. Oisin says yes, and leaves with her. They ride away from snow-bound Ireland and arrive at a land in full summer beauty. He lives happily with her. They have a daughter. One day, when his daughter is about 3, it hits him. He has been so lost in happiness that he's not sent so much as a message home! His father, Fionn, doesn't even know he's now a grandfather. He tells Niamh he wants to borrow the magic horse. She makes him promise never to dismount, not to let his body touch the soil of the land that gave him birth. Promise given, off he rides.

Reaching home, and riding to the top of the Hill of Almu, he finds no sign of his father and the warriors. He knows the Fianna move around but sees no sign that they intend to come back. Now he's troubled – has there been a great battle and he was not there to fight with, die with his friends, his father? He sees a little man below, struggling to lift a bale of hay. The hay is as big as the man but Oisin can't understand him making such a meal of it. He gallops down, grabs the hay with one hand, asks where it is bound and is told it is for the barn, over there. He throws it easily, then demands to know where are Fionn and the Fianna. The peasant doesn't understand. Oisin repeats the question, angrily. The peasant says, 'You don't mean those fellers from the old stories? Why, sir, nobody actually believes in them nowadays!' Oisin realises that time has passed differently where he was and that in his absence, centuries have passed.

He reaches for a second bale to cover his feelings, throws it, but doesn't set his weight right in the saddle. As the bale flies through the air, he falls. His body hits the ground and immediately all the centuries he has been away hit his body. He shrivels with age. The peasant calls a man, St Patrick, who arrives just in time to give Oisin the last rites.

So Oisin, in this story, journeys from this mortal world to a world of immortality and then returns to mortality and dies. Quite different from the happy homecoming, isn't it? No supper still warm by his bed. But I loved it when I was 14, and I love it now. Why? Well, isn't it true that we sometimes enter a wonderful world in our imagination and then are sad when, as the story ends, that world disappears? Have you ever read a book, watched a TV series, grown to love the characters and then been grieved that, now the story is over, you can no longer be with those people whose lives you have become so involved in, whom you have come to love? Have you ever felt there was a place and time in your life that you'd love to return to and felt the sadness that you can't, because even if the place is still there, the vanished time is not? I would suggest that this grief is a real grief and that, for a growing mind, it will mirror and model, in a safe way, experiences of loss and bereavement that any child will come to experience in their life. It's just like those young Israeli soldiers who had and hadn't been told scary stories as children, who could and could not handle real fear in real life.

I think my 14-year-old self, and not especially because I was 14, but just because that's when I happened to hear it, knew instinctively that there was something in this story that I needed. So, as you create Journey and Return stories for the child or children you are telling to, don't forget how important it can be to allow them to experience darker emotions too. So you can create it with them, and let them choose how dark things get.

But now for the recipe!

How to Make a Journey and Return Story

As you read these numbered steps, go back to your Memory Palace. Your Memory Palace is clear, as it was before you used it to remember the six stages of the Quest. You are going to make another one, this time to help you to remember the stages of Journey and Return. Before you do that, create an image in front of your first Memory Palace location, one that will symbolise Journey and Return. This way, when you call this image to mind it will help ensure all the other stages follow accurately. The stages are:

1. Who, Where, What Condition - *who is your story about, where do they live and what is their life like?*
2. Gateway - *who or what is going to serve to take them from their normal world to the world of their adventure? Does the Gateway come to them? Is it already in a familiar place, waiting to be discovered, or must they go to it?*
3. Journey - *your character is moved from their normal world to another world.*
4. New World - *where are they now? What is it like? What do they do? Who do they meet? Who are they in this new place?*
5. Gateway - *how are they going to be transported back home again?*
6. Return - *in what condition? With what feelings? With what changes of awareness?*

Have a go now at quickly creating the bones of a Journey and Return story. Tell it. How does it feel? Does it flow? Does it feel complete? Do events seem to follow one another in ways that, at least within the story, make sense?

Good. Now, do you want to kick it up a notch? Good! Now, may I tell you a story? A Journey and Return story to get you further into the mood?

Example Story – 'The Lad Who Had No Story'

In Scotland, many years ago, there lived a Laird who loved to throw parties. He liked these parties to include all sorts of people so you didn't have to be an aristocrat to be on the Laird's guest list, but you did need to have one thing. You needed to have a story.

Why? Well, at a certain point in the evening, when people had eaten more than they thought they could, and drunk more than they thought they should, the Laird would start gently banging a small gong. He started softly, but the sound grew. As his hall began, more and more, to fill with the throb of that little gong, people's eyes brightened. They smiled, they grabbed their seats, moved benches until they all sat in a circle. When they'd all arranged themselves, the Laird would hold up a small velvet bag and say, 'So what d'ye think's in here?'

'*Coins!*' the guests all cried.

'What sort of coins?' the Laird would ask.

'*Gold coins!*' the guests all called.

'And who d'ye think they're for?' the Laird would ask. 'Whoever tells the best story!' all the guests would chant, like schoolchildren, and they were all grinning like schoolchildren. They loved the Laird's parties and they loved the storytelling.

Next, the Laird began to pick people at random. He might not pick you, but if he did, you had to be ready to start your story straightaway. If people had already told before you, and if you were skilful, you could put things from other people's stories into your story, in a way that made it look like all the stories were connected (which, of course, they are).

The telling began, and young Mattie, a servant lad of about 19 years of age, who had never been to one of these gatherings before, leant close and lost himself completely in the beautiful stories.

One person told of a tailor who cheeked his Laird and had to, as punishment, go and sit in a certain haunted churchyard and sew a new pair of britches for the Laird at the stroke of midnight, when everyone knew the ghosts came out. It was funny. Someone else then told a story of a lad who didn't know what fear was, and cleverly had this lad stay the night in the same churchyard. And then someone changed it completely and told a story about a priest who preached in that very church who always said, 'Bless you!' to everyone he met and whose brother gave him a special horse that was trained to trot faster when the priest said, 'Bless you!' and stop when he said, 'Amen'. Mattie was having a lovely time.

Until the Laird said, 'Now then laddie, will you tell us a story?'

'Me?' said Mattie.

'Aye,' said the Laird, 'you.'

Mattie blushed. His stomach inside him seemed to lurch downwards. His mouth opened and closed, and then, 'But I don't have a story!'

Quite suddenly, nobody was smiling. The Laird was frowning.

'What?' said the Laird, sharply.

'I-I don't know any stories,' Mattie stammered.

The Laird leant forward. His eyes, which had been so twinkly, so friendly, now blazed with anger.

'You mean,' he said, very quietly, 'that you are happy to sit at my table, take the warmth of my fire, eat my meat, drink my ale, and you don't have anything to give me in return? You think that's all right, do you?'

'No sir ... sorry sir ...'

'Then get out!' said the Laird, 'and at least bring me something I want! I'm thirsty! Take this cup and fill it with some fresh water from the loch outside, but!' he said, raising one finger to show how much he meant this, 'I want clean, clear water from out beyond where the reeds and the rushes make it all mucky, d'ye hear me?'

Mattie leapt to his feet, grabbed from the Laird's hand a large pewter tankard, and ran out of the hall as fast as he could, his ears glowing.

Outside it was dark, no moon, no stars, but it was a soft, cool night. Moisture in the night air settled on Mattie's face, cooling his burning cheeks. He made his way carefully down the bumpy, stony path towards the shore of the loch. He tried to find a place where he could dip for water, but couldn't find anywhere he could reach beyond the reeds and rushes that fringed the shore until, up ahead, he made out the dark shape of a rowing boat moored at the shore.

'Good!' thought Mattie, 'If I can stand with one foot in that and one on shore I can reach further out!'

So Mattie planted one foot in the rushes, one foot in the boat. It wobbled in the water, but then grew still. He reached out, and then reached out just a little more. The next thing he knew, his right foot, the one in the boat, slid out and away from him. To stop himself from falling face first into the cold loch water, Mattie stepped forward with his left foot, so now both his feet were in the boat. And the boat slipped quickly away from the shore. It wasn't tied up at all!

Now Mattie was in a little boat that was sliding away from the shore. Mattie couldn't swim.

He looked around in alarm but then thought, 'It will stop drifting out soon, and I can call for help.'

But it didn't. Somehow, once it had started, the boat didn't stop at all. It seemed to have its own will, now that Mattie was in it, and he looked around himself again, now more in terror than alarm. The shore was, very quickly, getting further and further away and Mattie was surrounded by the glistening black waters of the loch. He looked over the edge. The water was already too deep for wading, and in any case, Mattie didn't fancy that cold, black water one little bit!

He looked forwards, in the direction in which the boat was travelling. Then he saw something that frightened him as much as the black water did. The boat was travelling with what seemed like its own momentum, towards an island in the middle of the loch.

Now everybody who lived around the loch knew this island, and everybody knew fine well never to go there. Everybody knew that this island, a small hillock with a few hawthorn trees rising out of the water, was a fairy island, that it belonged to the fairies, the little people, the good people. People called the fairies 'the good people' because they were scared of them and didn't want to accidentally offend them.

The boat was drifting faster, drawing closer. Mattie looked around the boat in desperation. Could he find anything to protect himself? No, apart from himself the boat was empty, not even an oar or paddle. He patted his trouser pockets, or tried to, but for some reason, he couldn't find them. His trousers seemed different. He went to pat the pockets of his shirt, because he might have his penknife stashed in there, or something, anything, but again, he found no pockets. But he did find something. He found something that gave him the shock of his life.

Because he found something under his shirt. The something he found was warm and soft. The something he found was him, only it wasn't him. He found, when his hands went to pat his chest, that he wasn't him anymore. He was now, unmistakably, her!

'Oh my Lord!' Mattie cried out, and his voice had changed too. It was lighter, softer. It was unmistakably a woman's voice. Mattie found he now had round hips, from which, not trousers, but a skirt hung. He had a soft bosom under his shirt. He had long, long hair. He was shocked. He was scared. He was she.

The prow of the boat hit that island and Mattie stumbled ashore. It was strange; from the shores of the loch, the island had looked like a little green hillock of an island with a few trees, but now that he was on it, it seemed much larger (I must stop saying 'he'! Now that 'she' was on it). The few trees were actually deep and peaceful woods. The ground spread out in large, soft meadows and, Mattie had never seen this from the shore, there were even houses.

Mattie stumbled towards one of the houses, one that had candles glowing in the windows. She was still holding the Laird's cup. The door opened and, as she came near, a very little old lady said, 'Come in, come in! You'll catch a chill being out so late!'

So Mattie did, and found a snug house with a good fire and some six or seven small people inside. They were mostly old women and old men but there was one young man who looked at Mattie very warmly, with bright, kind eyes. Mattie was puzzled at how nice it felt that he looked at her like that.

So Mattie stayed with these people. The oldest lady, with whom she spent much time, told her that once her people had lived around the shores of the loch; they'd lived, in fact, all over the country, but then new people had come and they'd all had to move to the island in the loch. The old lady's mouth set in a firm line when she said this, but then she smiled and asked Mattie to help with something, and Mattie did. Mattie found many tasks to help with and many tasks to do by herself. She slotted in to the life the small people had on the island very easily. Actually, they'd seemed small when Mattie first saw them but now they didn't, they just seemed the same sort of size as she was, only people said she was tall and that young man teased her. He said she had big feet. It was odd but, although she didn't like being told she had big feet, in a funny way she sort of didn't mind him teasing her. She liked him.

Actually, as time passed, Mattie realised she more than liked him. As time passed, she realised that she felt really happy when he was around. She learned that she felt really nice when he was looking at her, or just near her. And then, one evening, when they were all together by the fire, singing, he sat so close to her that their hands touched. Heart pounding, she didn't take her hand away.

The day they married was the happiest day of Mattie's life. Honestly! Her ears began to hurt from so much smiling. And such big, big smiles! He was smiling in the same way, everyone was. Mattie and her man moved together into their own, snug house and they lived together very well.

In time, Mattie and her husband had a child, a boy, and then, within the same year, twin girls. It was hard being parents because the children tested them, challenged them every day, almost every minute of every day. But neither Mattie nor her husband ever regretted having them. Their life was so full, and never the same. The children grew so fast and to see them learn, achieve, was the most exciting thing that Mattie had ever known. She was so proud of her family.

Then one day Mattie was in the old woman's house. The old woman, by the way, was her husband's grandmother, and Mattie loved her dearly. Grandmother was cooking a rich stew with meat and fragrant herbs, but she was frowning, because the stew was getting too dry. She reached for a large tankard and, turning to Mattie, she said, 'Be a love, will you, and fetch me some water from the loch? But not the mucky stuff at the edge, d'ye ken?'

It was a pewter tankard.

Mattie took it and walked to the shore. It was a beautiful day. Swallows were skimming the water, swooping and gliding. She could hear her daughters playing with their friends, and she knew her husband was teaching their son how to build a good wall with stones. She smiled as she walked to the shore, swinging the tankard by her side as she walked. Her eyes drifted over the island. She knew who lived here and who lived there and she knew exactly how every part of her happy life was mapped on this island, her home.

Reaching the shore, she saw the water at the shore was mucky with reeds, and the reeds were wearing strings of frogspawn. She wanted to reach further out. There was a boat moored at the shore. If she could plant one foot in the boat, leaving one on the shore, she could balance herself, and ...

And the same thing that had happened before happened again. The boat slid forward. Mattie stepped to prevent herself from losing her balance and found herself standing in a boat that was drifting fast, away from the island. She called and called but nobody heard her. She screamed her husband's name, she screamed and screamed for help, and nobody heard her. As she drifted away, it grew suddenly cold and suddenly dark, the water blackening around her. And when she looked down, she was no longer she. She was he.

Mattie reached the shore and staggered up the path to the Laird's hall. He burst through the door and everyone looked at him in surprise. Nobody was talking. Then the Laird said, 'I thought I told you to fetch some water?'

And Mattie burst out, 'Never mind the water! You've got to listen to me! I've just ...'

And Mattie told his story. Sometimes he smiled when he remembered his husband, their children, but when he told about drifting away from them his voice shook and his shoulders heaved. People listening dabbed at their eyes. When he'd finished, there was silence, and then a storm of applause and cheers. The Laird said, 'That's the best story I've ever heard. I don't believe anyone will better that tonight. Give the prize to Mattie.'

And Mattie found himself gazing blankly, stupidly, seeing a bag of coins and seeing nothing.

'But what about my wee'uns?' he said. 'My man? I've lost them all! I've lost my home!'

Folk in the hall looked at each other, then at Mattie in his distress.

'Mattie,' said the Laird, 'you must realise, you've scarcely been gone a minute!'

Advanced Journey and Return

The lovely thing about Journey and Return is that you can very easily nest another Form of Story inside it, using Journey and Return as a framing device.[23] For example, once your character has been transplanted into another world, they can go on a Quest (as the children do in *The Lion, the Witch and the Wardrobe*, or, for example, as Dorothy does in *The Wizard of Oz*). So your structure would now look like this:

1. Who, Where, What Condition - *who is your story about, where do they live and what is their life like?*
2. Gateway - *who or what is going to serve to take them from their normal world to the world of their adventure?*
3. Journey
4. New World
    - 4.1. Who, Where?
    - 4.2. Problem
    - 4.3. Journey
    - 4.4. Friend/Help
    - 4.5. Enemy/Obstacle
    - 4.6. Resolution
5. Gateway
6. Return

For example, the Problem could be the problem of getting home. Or it might be a completely different Problem associated with a completely different life in a completely different world (possibly more fun?). As you journey through this book you will meet other Forms of Story that you can just as easily nest inside the structure of Journey and Return, allowing you to take any character from anywhere and place them wherever you want. This is how a child can become a monarch in Narnia, how a Connecticut Yankee, in Mark Twain's glorious comic novel can, after a blow on the head (a handy Gateway device), find himself in King Arthur's Court in a novel that, by thus angling the mirror, can deeply reflect life in nineteenth-century America. You'll notice, when you nest a story inside another story your listeners will get so caught up in the internal narrative that they will almost forget the original. When they Return to it they will feel like they have travelled a very long way and they will feel a genuine pleasure and relief as they realise they are coming 'home'. Phew! Take a rest (I need one too after that sentence). Then try Journey and Return with a Six-Part Quest nested inside first. It's by far the easiest.

How did it go?

3

Rags to Riches

Are you ready for another one? This next Form of Story is one that should seem very familiar to you.

Rags to Riches is a very popular Form of Story. In this Form we meet a character in deprived circumstances. This deprivation can be economic, emotional, romantic or more. We get a view of what life was like before their deprivation began.[24] They meet a stranger who miraculously transforms their circumstances and suddenly they are rich. Life now seems perfect, but after a time there comes a crisis in which the new, exalted status is threatened. The character either passes the test and the story finishes with the riches confirmed or they fail the test and their story closes with the rags returned. 'Rapunzel' is a Rags to Riches story, and so too is 'Cinderella'. The 1980s Hollywood comedy *Trading Places*, with Eddie Murphy, is a Rags to Riches story. Almost every Hollywood rom-com is a Rags to Riches story in which the riches in question are the winning of, the possession of, love. Think of Julia Roberts in *Pretty Woman*. The wealth-bringing agent is Richard Gere's stockbroker and the threat to her new status is her doubt that he will really love a prostitute.[25] Charles Dickens' *Great Expectations* is a Rags to Riches story, with every move the story makes identical in structure to 'Cinderella'.

So, how do you make yours?

As before, we will start by cleaning our Memory Palace and getting ready to create new items. Now, you can, of course, think, 'Not now, can't be bothered, I'll just read on!' There's nothing at all wrong with that. But do bear in mind that this book aims to teach you how to 'conjure' a functional story as if from thin air, so you will need to commit this to memory at some point. What time can ever be better than now? Start before your first station in your Memory Palace (which is clear and empty at this stage) and create another image that will this time make you remember the words Rags to Riches and will also, when you come to use your Memory Palace, trigger the necessary stages of the Rags to Riches structure. Do this now.

Done? Great. Now let's meet the stages for which you need to create images at each of the stations of your Memory Palace. You will be creating six images at six locations in total:

1. Who, Where and in What Positive Condition previously?
2. Same person but now in far worse, much-reduced circumstances.
3. Agent of Change (Fairy Godmother, Handsome Prince, Magic Lamp/ Genie, Svengali).
4. Riches - deprived character enriched. Evoke new exalted life your character now enjoys.
5. Test - to new status. Can Pip help Magwitch out of England in time? Will the Prince find the owner of the glass slipper? Will Rapunzel find her now blinded lover?
6. Test passed - but how and with what success? Is it Riches confirmed or Rags returned?

Once you've successfully memorised the stages of this Form of Story, have a go and conjure one up. Tell it to someone. When you've done this once, start playing around, opening up and expanding what can be meant by the concepts of 'deprived' and 'rich'. It doesn't have to be money. It can be love, attention, justice, anything! One that very young children would immediately respond to would be a journey from not enough food to a wealth of food. Or maybe a child who has no toys meets the person who makes toys and becomes toy-rich? Didn't Roald Dahl do that one, or was that chocolate? When you've played with this Form of Story, we can move on to the next. We're really rattling along now, aren't we?

Example Story – 'Cinderella'

You know this one, which is good, because that will make it easier for you to spot the structure beneath the words as you read. But did you know that, worldwide, there are thought to be roughly 3,000 stories that follow this story structure and whose motifs are similar enough to be called versions of 'Cinderella'? I myself know of a Russian version, an Indian version in which the Prince is looking for the owner of not a glass slipper but a particular nose ring, and there are versions from Africa, from the South Pacific, from pretty much everywhere.

*Incidentally, many people think that the famous glass slipper is a slip of the tongue, or mistranslation, from French whereby fur (*fourrure*) became glass (*verre*). This could be true and is certainly more practical for dancing. Less likely is the authenticity of a West Country English version called 'Ciderella' in which the Prince tries to identify his true love by the precise purple of her nose. The version of 'Cinderella' that follows is adapted from the Brothers Grimm. I have swapped stages 1 and 2 around on purpose. Why? Well, to prove something that we have looked at already in Testing the Bones – that you can, if the posts of the story are strong enough, rearrange them at will and it will still make sense. We will return to this in more detail later in this book when we look at Four Types of Plot. For now, the story, adapted from the Brothers Grimm and other sources ...*

The young woman knelt on the floor and grasping the wet rag in her strongest hand, scrubbed and scrubbed until the floor tiles shone. Behind her, the fire burned, but the young woman couldn't feel its warmth. No, all that heat was absorbed by the bodies of her stepmother and her two stepsisters, who sat between the young woman and the fire. They had eaten their supper, roast goose with chestnuts, and now they were eating cream cakes. The young woman, who scrubbed and scrubbed while they scoffed and scoffed, would only eat when they'd all gone to bed and she would only eat the scraps. She would never sit close to a good fire but only next to the cinders when most of the fire had burnt out, and that's why they called her Cinderella.

It hadn't always been like this. Years before, Cinderella had lived with her father and her mother, and those had been such happy times that now she could run to them in her mind when the house was dark and quiet. She could remember her mother's lovely smile. She remembered the way her mother's eyes shone when she looked at her daughter, and she remembered her father laughing happily. Her father didn't laugh any more, and her mother was dead. This was the danger with memory – you couldn't just remember the things that made you happy without remembering the things that made you sad too. So, unavoidably, Cinderella remembered her mother in bed, in that bed she was never again to rise from. She remembered her mother's face all wasted and thin. But those eyes still shone when she took her daughter by the hand, saying, 'Soon, my darling, your mummy will die, but I promise I will watch over you from Heaven! Just plant a tree on my grave and, when you are in need, shake the tree and you shall get what you need.' Soon after that, Cinderella's mother did die. Cinderella did plant a tree on her grave. There was no need to water it – her tears were ample for that. Two seasons of growth and two seasons of snow passed over that little tree. Cinderella herself was growing into a young woman and her father, who loved her very much, thought, 'My girl is becoming a woman! There should be a woman in the house who can talk to her and tell her about things that I can't help her with.'

So he married again. He married a woman whose husband had died, a woman who had two daughters of her own. Now you might have heard that these two sisters were ugly sisters? They weren't! They were tall and graceful and beautiful, they were gorgeously attired. On the outside they truly looked like birds of paradise! But on the inside they were vultures. As soon as this woman and her daughters entered the house and as soon as they saw Cinderella, the temperature in the house dropped so sharply, plummeted so deeply that, even though it was summer, Cinderella pulled her shawl about her. This was the start of a new life.

'What's that girl doing in the best room? Remove her things at once! What's that girl doing with all those fine dresses, all those fine things? I will take those! She can wear a simple grey dress that will be appropriate for the work I have in mind for her. That's right Missie, work! Your days of lounging around reading catalogues are over! I won't stand to see your miserable face mooning around, you must work. Work!'

So from that day on, Cinderella wore only the shabbiest of clothes and Cinderella worked, while her stepmother and stepsisters lounged around, reading catalogues, trying on fine clothes. She got up before dawn, chopped wood, lit the fire. She carried pails of water and heated it for her stepmother and stepsisters to bathe with. She prepared their meals and cleared away and washed up after. She didn't go to the grave or speak to that tree because she couldn't bear to tell her mother how unhappy she was.

Right now, the stepmother and stepsisters were reading catalogues with even more than their usual avidity. They were choosing, ordering, trying costly dress after costly dress, and plumes and head-dresses and fascinators were fixed and unfixed in a frenzy of adornment. So too were all the women of that country, because they'd all heard that a great Ball was to be held at the Palace, and the Prince would be there! The stepmother and stepsisters were ordering Cinderella's father out of the house every day, forcing him to talk to people he used to know but with whom he hadn't spoken in years, to people he'd never met or didn't like, but talk he must to anyone who might be connected and who could get them an invitation.

One day, Cinderella saw her father come home, exhausted, drained, but also relieved, because he held in his hand invitations to the Ball. Four invitations. It goes without saying that there was no invitation for Cinderella. Cinderella's father's eyes looked to her in secret apology. He couldn't say anything, not now. There was no need. Cinderella looked at her father. She'd never seen those deep lines at the side of his mouth before.

The day came for the Ball. Upstairs, the stepsisters and stepmother were making themselves beautiful (though you wouldn't have thought them beautiful, not if you could hear the way they spoke to each other!). Cinderella's father was already dressed in the only good suit he had. It looked a little faded now; the black fabric had grown shiny with age and now looked almost greenish, like a glass bottle. He sat by the dwindling fire, looking glum. Cinderella was washing the pots. Then, the ladies came downstairs, all plumed and peacocked. For a moment, they looked dazzling, but within seconds the two sisters were scowling at each other and the stepmother was scowling at her husband.

'Bring the coach round!' she ordered, and Cinderella's father conveyed them all not to a coach, but to his cart, and he drove them to the Ball. Alone, Cinderella immediately felt it was easier to breathe. She breathed in, and in, then let it all out in one great big sigh.

At which there was a flash of light in the kitchen. Alarmed, Cinderella ran to the kitchen, and there stood a fairy. Cinderella knew she was a fairy! She wore green and such a tall, conical hat! The fairy said, 'Cinderella, why are you so sad?'

Cinderella couldn't speak. Where would she start? The fairy said, 'You needn't say anything! Go to your mother's grave and shake the tree and you will see what you will see!'

So Cinderella did as she was told and when she shook the tree, look! A beautiful gown appeared, brocaded, bejewelled and of the most finely tailored silk! She gasped, 'But what is this for?'

'Why,' said the fairy, 'so that you too may go to the Ball! Shake again!'

Cinderella shook again and as she did a large pumpkin at the corner of the garden was transformed into a fine carriage. Shaking more, six mice were transformed into six white horses with a seventh changed into a driver in a smart uniform. She shook once more, at every shake her smile of dazzlement growing wider (and more dazzling) and two smart and stripy lizards became two footmen in smart and stripy uniforms. She shook one last time and gasped, because there before her were a pair of the most beautiful shoes! They were elegant, they were graceful, they were made of glittering glass. Cinderella got dressed and, looking in her stepmother's mirror, she stumbled at the sight of herself.

'Now,' said the fairy, 'go to the Ball, dance with the Prince, and he will surely fall in love with you. *But!* Make sure you leave before the stroke of midnight because, when midnight comes, all this magic will reverse and everything shall be as it was before.'

She helped Cinderella into the carriage and she was driven to the Palace.

When she arrived and entered the ballroom, everyone gasped. Who was she? Men gaped at her beauty, women too. The stepmother and stepsisters gaped as well, completely winded by the arrival of this dazzling beauty, and, of course, they didn't recognise her as their drudge, Cinderella. They didn't even feel they might have seen her before somewhere. And the Prince! The Prince saw her and felt that he did know her. Something about her, he couldn't think where he'd seen her before, and couldn't understand why he didn't remember such a meeting more clearly, and yet, as he looked at this lady whose name he didn't know, he felt, in the strangest, deepest way, that he knew her! Looking at her, he felt like the music, the voices, were all suddenly much quieter and suddenly, he could hear, much louder, the rasp of his own breath and the thump, thump, thump of his own heart.

He went immediately to ask her to dance and that night, to the chagrin of every other woman present, he danced with nobody else!

'What's your name?' he asked her.

'What does that matter,' she answered, 'you will never see me again!'

'But I will!' he swore, 'I must!'

'But you won't!' said Cinderella, and there was such sweet sadness in her smile that the Prince thought her even more beautiful, even though he knew that wasn't possible. The Prince and Cinderella danced and danced, talked and talked. Cinderella was delighted! She'd imagined that a Prince would be stuffy, snobbish, self-important, self-interested, but he wasn't. He asked her so much about herself that she had to bite her tongue. She felt like she wanted to tell him everything and would only just remember in time that she couldn't.

Then, with a shock, Cinderella heard the big deep bell of the clock begin to toll the hour of midnight! *Bong!* Mid-dance, she broke from the arms of the Prince. *Bong!* She ran through the startled dancers. *Bong!* She dashed from the ballroom losing, in her haste, one of her beautiful glass slippers. *Bong!* She leapt into her carriage and ordered her team to drive and, pell-mell, they did. *Bong!* They made it round the corner. *Bong!* They galloped down the palace approach. *Bong!* They tore through the streets of the city and *Bong!* into the darkness of the countryside where, with no one to see them, *Bong! Bong! Bong!* they reverted abruptly to their former state. Two lizards and seven mice scattered off into the hedgerows and in the darkness a slim, shabbily dressed young woman carried a heavy pumpkin home.

The next day the stepmother and stepsisters were tired, cross and even more surly than usual. The Prince hadn't danced with either of the two stepsisters. He hadn't danced with anyone except that mysterious princess and, when she disappeared, the Prince disappeared too and it just wasn't the same without him.

'She was beautiful though ...' said one of the sisters.

'Yeah,' said the other, through gritted teeth, 'probably all fake!'

'Yeah,' said the first.

Cinderella, scouring a pan, smiled to herself. They were right, in a way.

The Prince had got up early that morning and summoned a meeting of all his staff. Some of them were a bit bleary-eyed, a bit foggy-headed, and they were bewildered by the energy of the Prince.

'Right, you chaps!' he said, 'I've got one, but we have to find its match!'

He was holding up the glass slipper that Cinderella had slipped out of as she fled. So off went all the Prince's men looking for that other slipper. They couldn't find it, so the Prince himself began the laborious process of visiting every household in his kingdom, asking all the women to try on the glass slipper.

Soon everyone in the kingdom knew of the Prince's search and one day, the stepmother called her daughters up to her room.

'Look here,' she said, 'here's what you must do! When the Prince comes here, which he must, if the slipper doesn't fit, just take this knife,' and here she produced a sharp knife with a hungry-looking edge, 'and cut off as much of your foot as you need to make your foot fit the slipper. It will hurt, a bit, but what's a little pain compered to marrying a prince?'

The stepsisters looked at the knife, nodded uncertainly.

'Just remember girls,' said their mother, 'if it doesn't fit, it's *your* fault.'

The day came when the Prince came to their door. The two stepsisters were hopeful, because they both had shapely, beautiful feet. The first sister tried and her foot nearly did fit! She swore that it did. The Prince hoped it didn't because, even though this young woman was beautiful, there was something he didn't like about her. She swore that it was a perfect fit so the Prince asked her to stand up in it, and she couldn't! She tried to take a step but she couldn't bear her weight on her foot, so much had she bunched it up to squeeze it in. Now she was standing, you could see the flesh of her foot swelling out of the slipper like the top of a muffin, and she was clearly in agony. The second sister said, 'I will try, but will you give me a moment?'

The Prince said he would, and she went upstairs to her mother's room. Meanwhile, Cinderella, in her filthy rags, tried to make herself as invisible as possible and shrank into a dark corner. She couldn't bear it if the Prince saw her like this!

Everyone heard a sharp yelp from upstairs. They all stopped talking in surprise. The stepmother, stepping close to the Prince, began talking very loudly to him, 'Your Highness, how do you like my flowers?'

She indicated a large vase.

'Do you like their arrangement? Is it not lovely? My daughter, who will be down in a minute, arranged them herself!'

Not true. Cinderella had done it.

'See how the pinks compliment the reds,' she went on, but she had to speak louder and louder because from upstairs, louder and louder yelps were becoming shrieks of pain, shouts of rage. 'And see now how the *reds compliment the deep crimson, because my daughter knows I dislike garish contrasts of colour, so pink, red, scarlet, crimson, even blood red, all assort together and ...'*

There came from above a scream so deafening that even the stepmother couldn't talk over it. The Prince and all his staff looked alarmed. Whatever next?

What next was the sound of someone hopping down the stairs. The door that stood closed at the bottom of the stairs now swung slowly open, revealing the oldest stepsister. Her face was flushed pink. Her pale frock was spattered with drops of, streaks of, scarlet, which even now were dying the pale fabric pink. She hopped on one foot, holding the other off the ground. It was crudely bandaged at the front and that bandage was already turning from white to crimson. There was no need to ask what she'd done and though she wanted to try the glass slipper the Prince would not permit it. He said he would leave now, and he was just leaving when he stopped abruptly.

'Wait,' he said, 'there's someone else!'

He was looking at the darkest corner of the room, where Cinderella was hiding.

'What?' said the stepmother, 'Oh, her! Don't bother, she's nobody!'

'Madam!' said the Prince, firmly, 'In my opinion, nobody is nobody!'

He stepped towards Cinderella, who shrank back, and back.

'You needn't be afraid!' said the Prince. 'Please don't shrink from me!'

Despite the gloom, the shadow, despite the shrinking, the cowering, there was something about this downtrodden woman that made the Prince want to lift her up. There was something about her that, when he looked at her, even though he couldn't quite see her, everything else around seemed quieter, seemed to recede and he could hear himself breathing. He felt as if he knew her from somewhere.

She stepped into the light and the Prince got a shock! He was sure he'd seen her before. This time, he was right. He knelt down and proffered the glass slipper and from under the dirty and the tattered rags that robed her, the young woman extended a beautiful foot, delicate and strong at the same time, the Prince thought. He took the foot gently in his hand and slipped on the glass shoe. It was a perfect fit!

'I knew it!' said the Prince, 'it's you!'

The Prince stood up, his hands seizing Cinderella by her upper arms, 'I knew it was you! I hoped it was you! It can only be you!'

The stepmother and the two stepsisters turned pale with horror, and then it got even worse for them because the Prince dropped to his knees before Cinderella. 'My lady, you are the dazzling princess I danced with at the Ball, you are the enchanting lady I spoke with at the Ball, you are the bewitching lady with whom I fell hopelessly in love at the Ball and for whom I have been looking ever since! Will you marry me?'

Cinderella could hardly speak but she managed to gasp out, 'Yes!'

So the Prince drove Cinderella away and the Prince was so happy, and Cinderella was so happy and Cinderella's father was the happiest he had ever been for years, and he was the proudest man in the kingdom when the Prince married his daughter, except for, perhaps, the Prince himself, and they all lived happily together until the end of their days.

The stepmother and her daughters were not happy, were never happy, but then, sadly, some people just don't have that gift.

4

Rebirth

Rebirth, in which a protagonist is established, then submerged under an evil influence and then reborn, is a beautiful and versatile Form of Story. You will find Rebirth in such classics as 'Sleeping Beauty' and 'Thorn Rose' (these are basically the same story, just French and German versions). You will also find Rebirth in contemporary films like Pedro Almodóvar's *Talk to Her*. *Talk to Her* is a very adult version of 'Sleeping Beauty'. It is typical of Almodóvar to put romance into such dark places but the thing that makes his comatose beauty awaken is actually exactly what happens in the Baroque French version of 'Sleeping Beauty' as collected by Charles Perrault (1628–1703). Not for the kids, that one.

The stories I've mentioned are some of the most intricately developed versions of this form, with a great deal of invention going into building complexity into the preliminary stages before the protagonist is submerged, but there are also simpler versions such as 'The Juniper Tree', or a version I tell that I know as 'Orange, Lemon and Lime' (I've never seen it written down so that title's as good as any other). In these simpler versions the protagonist is very quickly established and then just as rapidly submerged. Intriguingly, you will very often hear Rebirth-structured speech on the lips of people who are not storytellers; think of the 'Recovery from Addiction' story, or the 'Triumph Over Bad Beginnings' story ('I was raised in the streets. I was into all sorts of stuff and if it wasn't for Hip Hop/Jesus/the Duke of Edinburgh Awards Scheme I'd be dead or in jail by now ...'). Every 'Slimming/Getting Fit' story is a Rebirth story. One thing that muddies perception of this form is that you can have stories in which characters are reborn or released from a curse but are they the main protagonist? For example, the Prince in 'Rapunzel' is blinded and then healed but is he the main character? No, Rapunzel is, so that has to be her Rags to

Riches (similarly in 'The Frog Prince' and in 'Snow White') story. There's nothing stopping anyone from retelling the story of Rapunzel but positioning the Prince as protagonist and then it *would* be a Rebirth story.

Let's make one now for ourselves.

Get ready to build another Memory Palace and start by creating, before the first station of your Memory Palace, an image that will make you remember the word 'Rebirth'. Done? Now let's start the Rebirth story Memory Palace. It's a powerful template because we are all aware, even when we are young, that our lives can become seriously overcast, that we can simply become the victim of terrible misfortune and we hope that we can, in such circumstances, be miraculously restored to happiness. I told you earlier in this text of the little girl I told stories to in hospital who asked, every week, for the same story? It was 'Orange, Lemon and Lime', a Rebirth story. Small wonder she, who had been so badly hurt, longed for stories of restoration from the injuries that held her down. My own story of sight loss at 25, serious illness and disability and then recovery, thanks to my wife, to storytelling, voice teaching, etc. fits without effort into the Rebirth story structure.

So:

1. Who, Where and in What Positive Condition?
2. Negative Agent of Change - a wicked stepmother? An angry fairy? A tyrant? A bottle? An act of carelessness?
3. Submersion of Protagonist - under a curse, 100 years of sleep, a coma, dictatorship, addiction, obesity?
4. Positive Agent of Change - a handsome prince, a rehab sponsor, a compassionate teacher?
5. Rebirth - into new and exalted life.

Example Story – 'Thorn Rose'

Many years ago, in the green and golden land we now call Germany, there lived a Lord and his Lady wife. They were very happy together. They were very good and kind to the people who lived in their lands or who worked for them and so all of their domain was very happy. They were such fine people that even the fairies were happy to live in their lands.

Now, for a long time, even though they really wanted one, the Lord and his Lady had no child. When, one year, the Lady realised that she was expecting a baby, people were very excited, but none more so than the Lord himself. After what seemed the longest wait, and yet which seemed to fly by, the Lady went into labour and she gave birth to a lovely little girl. The Lord and the Lady were both thrilled with their daughter, and they named her Rose.

The Lord decided to throw a big feast to celebrate the birth of their daughter and he began to make the arrangements. He had already invited many important people and he was just inviting the fairies, when his wife said to him, 'But darling, wait! There are thirteen fairies living in our lands and we only have twelve gold plates!'

The Lord stopped. He knew exactly what she meant. I'm sure you do too, because, of course, fairies will only eat from a golden plate. What could they do? Well, the Lord solved the problem quickly enough; 'Never mind!' he said, 'we'll just invite twelve fairies.'

The day came for the feast and all the guests were arriving. All the guests bowed and thanked the Lord and the Lady. All the guests queued up to approach the cot where the baby, Rose, was lying. They all congratulated the Lord and Lady, said what a lovely baby Rose was and all wished her a happy life. The Lord and Lady beamed with pride.

Then people gasped in wonder. The first of the fairies had arrived. Even though everyone knew that fairies lived in the land, it didn't mean that anyone had ever seen them! They were too mysterious, too magical. But there she was, the first fairy. Nobody could move and they were all speechless. The fairy, in her long gown, in her tall hat, carried her long, thin wand as she moved through the crowd. You had to say 'moved', you couldn't say 'walked', because nobody could see her body doing anything as ordinary as walking. She just glided from the entrance of the hall to the cot where Princess Rose lay. Princess Rose also stopped gurgling and gazed, her eyes shining with wonder, as the first fairy leant over her cot, and said, 'I bless this child with the gift of good health!'

All the people applauded, and then the second fairy arrived. She blessed the baby Rose with the gift of happiness, and the third fairy gave her the gift of song, the fourth the gift of intelligence, the fifth the gift of laughter, the sixth the gift of wisdom, the seventh the gift of beauty, and so it went, with each fairy bestowing a gift on the baby, the people applauding and the Lord and Lady beaming from ear to ear, happier than they could ever imagine. It went on. The eleventh fairy was just giving Rose the gift of confidence, when suddenly the door of the hall burst open. There was a gust of cold wind so icy it made everyone shiver. A flurry of dried leaves, all crinkled and brown, swirled into the room, even though it was summer, and with them came the thirteenth fairy. She'd heard about the great feast, she'd realised she wasn't invited and she was furious!

No one could move as she swept into the hall. No one could stir as she flew up to the Lord, the Lady, their smiles frozen and then, turning to the cot and little Rose, she said, 'And I have come to give my gift! My gift is this. On her eighteenth birthday, when she is in the first full flowering of her beauty, Rose will prick her finger on a needle and she will *die*!'

And with that, the thirteenth fairy swept her tattered robes about her and flew out of the hall. People were stunned. The Lord and Lady, stupefied, clutched each other by the hand. This was a disaster! But the twelfth fairy had not yet wished. She spoke clearly, so everyone would hear, 'I cannot entirely undo my sister's angry wish. My magic is not strong enough. But I can soften it. When she reaches 18 Rose must prick her finger on a needle but she will not die. Instead, she will fall asleep for a hundred years!'

With that, the twelfth fairy and all the other fairies left. All the guests left, leaving the Lord and Lady now so tiny in an immense and empty hall, staring in disbelief at their even tinier little daughter. To sleep for a hundred years? Why, that was as good as death to them, because they would lose her!

But the Lord wasn't a lord for nothing. He was intelligent, resourceful and decisive. The next day he published a proclamation throughout his land that all needles, all spindles and all spinning wheels were forbidden and they were to be brought to his castle. Nationwide, there was a needle amnesty and hundreds of glittering needles were melted down and turned into spoons. The spinning wheels, their pedals and treadles and wheels, were all piled up in a huge pile in front of the castle and they were burnt. The fire was so big it burnt all of that day and late into the night and the Lord and Lady saw in those licking flames their daughter's safety. How could Rose prick her finger with a needle if there wasn't a needle in the land? The textile industry was destroyed but the Lord did his best to find other work, other trades and appropriate retraining for those affected, and he was reassured that his daughter now could grow in safety.

Rose did grow, she grew fast and it was obvious to all who met her that all the fairies' many gifts were truly given because she was healthy, she was happy, she was joyful, intelligent, curious, sagacious beyond her years and she grew very beautiful. The Lord and Lady basked happily in the glow of their wonderful daughter and, in time, they and everyone else kind of forgot about that thirteenth fairy.

Then one day, it was Princess Rose's eighteenth birthday. People marvelled at her. Year on year she had grown more lovely, more kind, more wise, more beautiful and now, at 18, she really was no longer a pretty girl but a wonderful young woman. There was to be a great feast for her birthday later that day and servants were running around decorating the castle. Down in the kitchens the servants were working, urgent to prepare all the food. So Rose was all alone and wandering happily around the castle when she walked past an open door.

She never normally noticed that door. It was usually closed and behind it were some stairs that didn't go anywhere very interesting, only on this day, as Rose walked past, she stopped, intrigued by a distant whirring and clicking noise. She opened the door a little further and poked her head inside. The noise was coming from up that spiral staircase. She wondered what it could be?

Well, one of the fairies had gifted Rose with intelligence and you can't be intelligent without being curious, and so Rose wanted, more than anything, to know what was making that interesting noise. She began, quietly, to climb the spiral stone staircase.

Up and up she climbed until she came to a small room. Every step she climbed the noise grew louder and louder. And then she saw the strangest sight she'd ever seen. In the room at the top of the stairs sat an old lady all dressed in a tatty black robe, and she was sat at the strangest and most interesting thing Rose had ever seen! There was a wooden seat, and the old lady's foot was going up and down, up and down, and a great wooden wheel was whirring and whizzing round. The old lady turned her head, her old face wrinkled into a wide and happy smile;

'Hello, my dear!' she said, 'Come in!'

So Rose went in.

Rose was fascinated! The old lady held a cloud of soft wool in her right hand. Her foot worked the treadle. The wheel span and as the old lady pulled at the cloud of soft wool she twisted with her skilful fingers and fine yarn just appeared! All at once, and for the first time, Rose realised where every stitch of clothing she had ever worn came from, and she was delighted!

'Do you want to have a try?' the old lady asked. Rose did. She picked up the spindle the old lady indicated and began to turn it in her hand. She turned it and turned it and suddenly, ouch! She pricked her finger on the sharp tip of the spindle. The fairy's curse from all those years ago came true as Rose fell down as if dead; she dropped into a heap on the floor. The old woman threw back her head and cackled. She swept her tatty black robe about her, sending a flurry of crinkly brown leaves around the room, and she flew out of the open window.

Rose was not dead, but she had fallen so deeply asleep that you'd think she was if you saw her. It wasn't just Rose. The instant Rose fell asleep, her mother and father, sat downstairs in their hall receiving visitors, fell asleep. The visitors fell asleep. All the servants decorating the castle for the feast fell asleep. Ribbon and tinsel hung from their apparently lifeless hands. In the kitchen, the Lord's butler, who had just been about to sneak a sip of his master's best wine, fell asleep with the glass halfway to his mouth. The cook had just caught one of the kitchen boys stealing a jam tart and was just about to box his ears. Both cook and kitchen boy fell fast asleep. The woman turning the spit to roast the goose fell asleep. The flames fell asleep. Another lady, who'd been plucking the goose, fell asleep and the goose feathers fluttered slowly to the floor. Outside, guards fell asleep standing, leaning on their spears, their helmets slumping on their heads. Dogs fell asleep in their kennels, horses in their stalls. All the busy motion of that great castle was hushed! It stopped, slumped, slept soundly and silently. That wasn't all. Around the castle, the soil began to crack and split and whoosh! Great thick briars and thorns began to grow up and up and around the castle. They twisted, they writhed, they wound and knotted themselves so tightly and thickly about the castle that soon you couldn't see so much as a stone of it! You would see only a great green hedge, spiky with thorns, and then, equally suddenly, beautiful, deep red roses began to open all over that green cage. The castle was entirely hidden in roses.

Somehow, news spread around the continent of the beautiful Princess Rose lying asleep in a spellbound castle. Young princes heard this story and thought to themselves that they must find this haunted place, cut their way in, free the princess and marry her. Well, they'd grown up hearing stories about this kind of thing – small wonder they were ill-prepared for life. So they climbed on horses, rode the lands, looking. Some of them found the castle, saw the thickness of the briars and gave it up as a bad job. Some of them didn't make it to the castle at all because they found something else that interested them on their way there. Some found the castle, wrapped in its fragrant cage and they frowned. Inside there, they knew, was their princess, but how would they get in?

First one arrived, drew his sword and began to hack his way through the rose briars. He got a certain way in but the thorns snagged at him, plucked his clothes, pierced his skin. Cursing and swearing, he hacked and cut but soon found the briars so thick he could make no further progress. He tried to turn round, to turn back, but the briars he had cut through had grown again behind him, closing him in. He couldn't get out. The next prince to arrive, weeks later, saw the first prince, his body wrapped in briars like a fly wrapped in a spider's web and just as dead. The third prince saw the second and first thus cocooned, the fifth saw the fourth, the twenty-ninth saw the twenty-eighth, the forty-seventh saw the forty-sixth and so on and so on until, when the eighty-third arrived he saw the hedge of roses hung with the bodies of princes, some now many feet off the ground (because the hedge kept growing) and he thought better of it. After him, no further princes came. People talked about the Princess Rose for a few more years and then it all got forgotten. The briars grew thicker, the roses smelt sweet and, somewhere inside, the Princess Rose and everyone else slept and slept.

Ninety-nine years passed. Towards the end of the ninety-ninth year a young Prince was riding around the country. He wasn't looking for the castle, indeed, he'd never heard of the castle, but was just looking about himself because he knew that he was just at that brief and beautiful time, when the limitations of childhood had been released and the responsibilities of adulthood were yet to be borne. Beautiful, we know, and brief as the season of a single rose. One day, in his riding, he came to the most extraordinary sight, a huge, tall, thick briar hedge covered in the most beautiful roses. He halted his horse and stared in amazement, taking in the sight, breathing in the fragrance. He was so lost in the wonder of this that when the tall lady spoke to him he was startled; he hadn't heard her approach.

'That's where the princess and all her household are lying, fast asleep!'

The Prince looked at this woman, tall and strong in a long gown, with a tall hat on her head. For some reason she held a long, thin wand of ash wood over her shoulder. The Prince asked what the lady meant. The lady told him of Princess Rose, cursed and trapped for a hundred years, held by the spell of the thirteenth fairy.

The Prince looked at the stunning display of roses and immediately thought of his own life, his liberty, his freedom to rove and to ride about the lands howsoever he wanted and he felt so sad for the Princess Rose. 'Poor lady,' he thought, 'to be so shut out from all of life, to be imprisoned so in beauty!' Suddenly, he dismounted from his horse and began walking towards the roses. Without quite knowing why, but thinking only how terrible it must be to be trapped in there, he strode towards that thicket of briars. He drew his sword.

But on this day, a hundred years had passed since the Princess Rose pricked her finger and fell into her swoon. Come the man, come the moment; come the moment, come the man! As the Prince lifted his sword to strike at the briars, those briars peeled back, rolled back, opening like a door, opening a spiny corridor for him. The Prince walked in and further in, led by the opening briars.

He came to the courtyard. There were the dogs fast asleep in their kennels, the horses in their stalls. There were the soldiers slumbering in their sentry boxes and all the busy people stopped as if dead in the middle of their comings and goings. The Prince went inside the castle. He saw the Lord and Lady fast asleep, their visitors fast asleep. Without quite knowing why, he began to climb that spiral staircase. He climbed to the very top and there he saw her!

The open window that the old lady had flown out of now had roses growing through it, flowing through it like a crimson river. The Prince saw how the roses had grown beneath and around the Princess Rose. He feared the thorns must be hurting her, but saw, to his amazement, that all the thorns had turned away from her, only facing outwards, never inwards. The briars held her off the ground and she lay as if in a soft bed. The Prince looked at her and felt as if all the world was focussed here, that all light shone only to illuminate her face. Her skin was so pale and soft! Her lips were so red. Rose red. Gently, reverently, he kissed her. She woke smiling without knowing why she smiled, and when the Princess Rose awoke all the castle awoke. Her mother and father awoke in their chairs, their visitors awoke and continued what they were saying. The woman resumed plucking the goose. The spit turned, the flames roasted, the butler sipped his Lordship's wine, the cook boxed the kitchen boy's ears, the castle courtyard was busy again with all the comings and goings of life, the soldiers stood to attention, the horses stamped and shook their heads and the dogs barked for no other reason than that they were dogs and felt like barking. And in that same instant, the Princess Rose, on her hundred and eighteenth birthday, fell deeply in love with the Prince whom she had never met before, and yet she couldn't imagine how she could ever be without him.

Example Story – 'The Lindworm'

By now, stories of young women falling placidly in love with men they've never previously met may be getting on your twenty-first-century nerves? Traditional stories, all stories perhaps, are in some way normative and sometimes we grow uncomfortable with the norm. We can also grow uncomfortable with a story or stories that support that norm. For this reason, and also to show how different a story can be even when it is based on the same structure, I offer another Rebirth story with a far more active female protagonist. This story does some interesting things with structure and we'll look at that afterwards. I tell this to children of 8+ and it is also one of my wife's favourites. I know it can be found in one of the many Langs' Fairy Books *but I can't tell you which one. I learned it orally, told by Christine McMahon.*

Many years ago, there was a Queen. She and her husband, the King, were very happy together. They loved and cherished each other and, when work was over, liked nothing more than each other's company. The King was loving and generous with his Queen and so she had lots of beautiful dresses, jewels, necklaces, tiaras and much, much more. Because she didn't just have tiaras, she had crowns. She didn't just have dresses, she had gowns. She didn't just have storytellers, she had singers and musicians and jugglers and acrobats and jesters and poets and clowns, and all to make her happy. Which she was. Except, there was one thing missing. Can you guess what it was?

That's right, a child. Despite how dearly they loved each other, despite how nearly they clasped each other, despite how clearly they both wanted their happy marriage to be blessed with a child, it wasn't. No child came and every month brought the Queen a crushing sense of failure, of disappointment, of despair. Because it wasn't simply that she wanted a baby - she knew it was her duty to provide the King with a son and the kingdom with an heir.

So as ruler of the kingdom, the King could afford doctors, and doctors came and examined and tested and tutted and humphed. They took pints of blood from the Queen. It didn't help. They put leeches on the Queen. It didn't work. They took glass jars, turned them upside down, passed a flame beneath them and stuck them, like limpets, on to the Queen's back but, and I know this will surprise you, that didn't work either. That month too brought that crushing sense of failure.

Despairing of doctors, the King tried wizards. Each one seemed intent on outdoing the other in the strangeness of their appearance, the scariness of their spells, the nastiness of their concoctions, but all of them failed. The King, secretly, was thinking about giving up.

Now, one of the reasons why the Queen was such a good ruler and so well loved was that she really did listen to everybody she could. So she listened to her servants and she heard them talking about what they did when they had a problem they couldn't solve. She learned that they went to see somebody they called the Wise Woman. The Queen learned that this Wise Woman, also known as the Hen Wife, lived in the woods, all alone, and if you needed her help you had to go to her cottage and ask for it. You had to pay her, and the Wise Woman liked to be paid in whisky. The Queen learned, from her servants' talk, that if your vegetables weren't growing, go to the Wise Woman. If you'd a dispute with a neighbour or a member of the family and you wanted it to smooth out, go to the Wise Woman. If there was somebody you liked, and they didn't even notice you, go to the Wise Woman, and the next time they saw you their eyes would be starting out of their heads like hat pegs in the chapel porch. So the Queen resolved to do something very brave. A few days later, she left her palace.

Of course, she'd left her palace before, but whenever she left the palace she had an armed escort. She would be in a coach and four, with soldiers on horseback to the front, to the back and at both sides of her. Soldiers went on ahead and whole streets were cleared for the Queen to come down, so whenever the Queen was in the city, the city was kept at a distance, and a hollowed-out orange skin filled with port wine and spices was enough to keep the smells of the city at a distance too, as she smelt only the aroma of citrus and wine and cinnamon. But this time was different. The Queen took off her crown, her jewels, her make-up and any other sign that she was royalty. She took off her rich robes and put on the linen clothes the serving women wore and her delicate skin was shocked at the itch and scratch of it. Looking as ordinary as she could, she left the palace by a little back door, and now she was really in the city.

And the city was in her face! People pushed her, jostled her, barged her, and the Queen almost screamed with the shock of it. The city smelt ripe. It smelt of spilt beer, of sweat, of rotten fish, of rancid meat and sour vegetables. People shouted, shouted so close to the Queen's ears that it hurt, and their speech was so rough the Queen felt she almost saw rocks and dirty coals coming from their mouths, not words. But she pressed on – she had to.

She forced her way through the heave of it, through the turbid streets and into the fields. She had never before realised how muddy fields were, nor how rutted and uneven the paths. It was so *hard!* But she had to. If she was ever going to have a baby, she had to. On and on she walked until she was deep in the woods and she was looking at a cottage, the Wise Woman's cottage.

To look at, it looked lovely. Peaceful it was, nestled into a clearing deep in the woods, with smoke lazing out of the chimney pot. But the smoke wasn't behaving properly – it kept changing colour. Now it was grey, now blue-grey, green-grey, green and red and gold. Now it was belching thick and black, now it was rising up, now it flowed downwards from the chimney pot as thick as oil, and the Queen wanted to run away! But she'd come this far. She stroked her tummy and knocked at the door.

'*Come in!*' a scratchy voice called, so, nervously, the Queen opened the door. Inside, the cottage was snug and warm, but it was dark too. The Queen took a few nervous steps inside and the door swung shut behind her. Looking down, the Queen saw one of the rugs had rucked up and she could see strange symbols, made of bright metal, hammered into the floor. Looking around, the Queen saw, on shelves that went all around the room, large glass jars that had things in. One had what looked like a tadpole, but as big as a rabbit. One looked like a lamb with all its skin pulled off. One looked like ... actually, the Queen didn't want to know what that looked like.

The Wise Woman, looking up, recognised the Queen right away but, just as she was greeting her in surprise, she also realised that the Queen did not want to be recognised and so, instead of 'Your Majesty!', said something more like, 'Your Maj-dam, madam, you're more than welcome! Sit down, why don't you, and make yourself comfortable?'

The Queen could sit down, but she couldn't make herself comfortable. She was far too frightened. The Wise Woman came and sat down too, and said, 'When you're ready and you're comfortable, perhaps you'd like to tell me what you've come to see me about?'

That was it. That was all that was needed, and the whole story, the whole sad, sorry story came spilling out of the Queen's lips. Her words were like lambs that have been cooped up too long inside and suddenly the barn is opened and they can smell fresh grass. Her words came leaping, tumbling, rushing out of her mouth, just like lambs. Except there wasn't any joy in them.

When the whole story had been told, the two women just sat there.

'I'm sorry,' said the Queen, 'I've ruined your hankie.'

The Wise Woman just shook her head – that didn't matter. Then the Wise Woman asked the Queen, 'Are you good at following instructions?'

'I think so?!'

'I'm going to give you something and, if you follow my instructions and if God is willing, you will have a child.'

The Queen gasped, her eyes wide.

The Wise Woman got up, opened a deep drawer and rummaged, then closed it again and opened and ransacked a cupboard. She came back to the Queen with a wooden box, kind of like a shoebox. She gave it to the Queen, who opened it and blinked. Inside were two fruits, or at least the Queen thought they must be fruit, but they were the strangest fruit the Queen had ever seen. One was soft like fruit, but so smooth it had no sign of either stalk or stem. When the Queen held it up and turned it round its colour changed from deep red to purple to blue to green to gold. The other fruit was all spikes and spines, warts and welts and, to be honest, it looked like it might eat you, not you it! The Wise Woman was talking to her, saying that she should, when she got home, run a bath so hot it was as if she was going to wash the clothes. Then, even as hot as that, she should get in and wait, wait until the water had gone from much too hot to too hot, from too hot to hot, from hot to warm, from warm to tepid, from tepid to cool, from cool to cold to 'oh my God I'm freezing'! And only when her teeth were chattering in her head and she couldn't feel her fingers and toes, she should reach for the first of the two fruit, peel it, eat its flesh, then do the same with the other, and she would have a child.

The Queen took the box. She gave the Wise Woman a bottle of whisky so superior that the Wise Woman was still looking at it in astonishment when the Queen left the cottage. She rushed back to the palace as fast as she could and ordered her servants to make a bath for her but to make it so hot that it was as if they were going to wash the clothes. Some of the servants looked a bit unsure about this but the Queen commanded them, and when a Queen commands ... she must have been reading one of her magazines, they thought, and did as they were told. They did it so well that there was so much steam in that bathroom that the Queen couldn't even see where the bath was. One of her servants took her by the arm and led her towards it. Once she had her hand on the edge of the bath the Queen knew where she was. She put the fruit at one end of the bath, stripped and got in.

Or tried to! It was so hot! But little by little, she did it. She didn't inch her way in, she half-inched. She didn't half-inch her way in, she centimetred, she millimetred her way in! Once in, she daren't move, or she would scald herself. She lay there, panting like a dog, staring at those fruit, and she waited until the water went from much too hot to too hot, from too hot to hot, from hot to warm, from warm to tepid, from tepid to cool, from cool to cold to 'oh, my God, I'm freezing!'

She was, and her teeth were chattering in her head. She grasped the first of the two fruit. She tried desperately to peel it but her fingers were too cold and so eventually she just crammed it into her mouth and ate it whole. The flesh, once she got to it, was sweet and lovely but the skin was tough and horribly bitter. Then she grabbed the other fruit. This one was easier, so she peeled it and ate it. She leapt out of the bath. Her servants wrapped her cold body in hot towels and massaged some warmth back into her. They were looking at her quizzically so the Queen said something about it being good to try these things but she didn't think she'd try it again.

A month passed and nothing.

Six weeks passed, and still nothing, but she didn't say anything. Eventually, when twelve weeks had passed and still nothing, and then one of her servants said, politely, that she might have to let out some of the Queen's dresses, then that was when she said something. She went to her husband and said to him, 'Darling? We are going to have a baby!'

The King was so happy! He embraced his wife so tightly, saying again and again in her ear that she was so clever, that he loved, he adored her. Then he went and told everybody. In the months that followed, everyone could see it. The Queen was pregnant, and getting bigger and bigger! The King told her she just got more and more beautiful, but that's not at all how she felt. She felt heavy and tired, her feet hurt and she had to keep going to the bathroom. But she could feel tickles and kicks inside her, and that was exciting!

In time, her time came and she was confined with only one midwife, the Royal Midwife, an old lady who, years ago, had even helped the King come into the world. The King paced up and down outside, and every sound he heard from inside wrenched at him. There were quite a lot of sounds! After what seemed an unending ordeal, the Royal Midwife said to the Queen, 'That's it your Majesty! I can see the baby's head now! Push!'

Push? What did the woman *think* she was doing?

Then the Queen had the most extraordinary feeling - she felt something leaving her body. Then the Royal Midwife said, 'Seconds away, your Majesty, Round Two! There's another one coming!'

'Oh, my God!' the Queen gasped, a great spasm squeezed through her body, she felt something else leave her and then a great wave of pain and exhaustion submerged her. When she surfaced, the midwife was smiling, 'Congratulations, Your Majesty! You've had a son!'

Something warm and soft was put into her arms and, smelling him, feeling him, holding him, the Queen fell so deeply in love with her son! He snuggled in and, immediately, began to drink her milk. The Queen looked up, 'But you said there were two?'

The Royal Midwife was holding something wrapped in a towel. She looked grim.

'Sometimes, Your Majesty, sometimes babies don't come out right. I don't think this one is going to live through the night.'

The Queen was stunned, 'But may I hold them?' she asked.

'I wouldn't advise it, Your Majesty, best to think only of the healthy child and not to get attached to this one. It will hurt less.'

But the Queen was not used to being told she couldn't do something and, in any case, it was her child! She reached for the towel the Royal Midwife was holding and tugged; and then she screamed! She screamed, because what the Royal Midwife was holding was not a child, or at least not a human one! The Royal Midwife was holding a worm. I don't mean a wriggly worm, an earthworm, I wish I did! It was a worm in the Old English meaning of the word, meaning a lizard, a serpent, a dragon. It was maybe a foot long. It was covered all over with hard, glittering scales. It had sharp teeth, sharp claws, oily green eyes and a crest of spikes and spines that went all the way down its head and neck and all the way down its back to its tail.

When the Queen screamed it opened its mouth, showing all its pointy little teeth, and hissed! The midwife dropped it and this Lindworm skittered across the floor, leapt up on to a stone balcony, turned, hissed again and then leapt out and off into the moat below.

'Oh my God!' said the Queen, 'I didn't see that!' And then, to the Royal Midwife, 'You didn't see that either!'

'No, Your Majesty, I didn't see that! I didn't see anything!'

So the King met one child, his son, and he was overjoyed. He took the boy and showed him to his barons and they too were overjoyed. Everyone was overjoyed. The King and Queen were parents now and their son, the Prince, grew.

He grew so fast! Have you heard that expression, don't run before you can walk? He could. He could sing and play instruments before he could talk, he could paint before he could chalk, he could hunt, shoot, trap and fish before he could stalk! His fencing master told the King the boy was the best student he'd ever had. 'I fancy he gets that from me!' said the King. His riding master, who taught him how to ride horses, said he was the finest young horseman he'd ever taught. 'I fancy he gets that from me!' said the King.

'He's so beautiful,' said the palace women, 'and so intelligent too!'

'Hmmph!' said the King, 'That's from his mother.'

The boy grew into a magnificent young man. The King and Queen aged, the King, in particular, thickening as he was around the middle and thinning as he was up top, that it seemed as if all their beauty, their youth, was leaving them and passing on to their son. Both parents watched him proudly. Then, one day, when the Prince was about 23, he said to the King, 'Father, I'm getting to an age where I ought to start thinking about settling down, about getting married. What do you think?'

'I agree,' said the King, 'but you're not to rush this! Your mother and I took our time to decide who we were going to be with and I'm sure that's one of the reasons we've both been so happy together. But, as it happens, I've been making some enquiries and in our neighbouring kingdom, you know where I mean, there just happens to be a princess about whom I've heard very good things. Take a horse, they're expecting you at any time.'

So the Prince did and, as he rode, asked himself, how would he know? Would it be obvious, like a thunderclap, or would it be stealthy, like the new leaves coming in April? He was so busy thinking these thoughts that he didn't notice his horse was getting nervous.

It was though. As he rode deeper and deeper into the thick forest that separated the two kingdoms, his horse had begun to nicker and whinny and now it was tossing its head and trying to turn off the path. The Prince didn't let it, but his hand went to the hilt of his sword, just in case. Might it be wolves? Or a bear? The bear would regret the day it crossed his path if it meant to do him harm ...

The next thing he knew his horse was bucking and kicking beneath him and it was all the Prince could do to keep his seat in the saddle. But he did, and his sword flashed out of its scabbard, because looming up in front of him, blocking his way, was an enormous Lindworm. It had grown just as the Prince had grown, and now it was 40 or 50ft long! It was clad all over in an armour of glittering scales! Its teeth were as long as a man's arm, and much thicker, and yet so sharp as could cut a human hair, lengthways!

'*You shall not marry!*' hissed the Lindworm, '*I must marry first!*'

'What do you mean you must marry first?' said the Prince.

'*It is the law!*' the Lindworm shrieked. '*The youngest son must not marry until the older son is married first!*'

'What do you mean "the older son"?' asked the Prince.

'*Go and ask your mother!*' screeched the Lindworm. '*Go and ask our mother!*'

The Prince couldn't go on, so he had to go back. Reaching the palace, he sought out his mother. She was surprised; wasn't he off to meet the Princess Thingummyjig? The Prince took her into a private room and told her what had happened. Poor woman. She went as white as milk and had to be helped to a chair.

'I've prayed,' she said, 'this day would never come!'

But it had, and so they had to tell the King.

The Prince had already told his mother he forgave her – without her actions he wouldn't have been born in the first place, and the King swiftly did the same.

Both father and son hugged the Queen until she believed them. The King said he needed to consult his advisors.

The advisors, once they'd heard the case, frowned and all fell into a ponder. 'Hmm!' they all said, and three days later they were still at it, pondering. Eventually, they said to the King that, legally speaking at least, the Lindworm was correct. It was the law of that country that the younger son could not marry until the older son had found a wife. It would be necessary to find a wife for the Lindworm and, notwithstanding the fact that he was a monster, he was a monster of the royal blood, and so it was necessary to find a princess who would marry the Lindworm. Notices were sent out to kingdoms far and wide, asking if anyone had a daughter of royal blood and marriageable age who would like to be married to the oldest son of the King of ... Certain details, as I'm sure you can imagine, were omitted. A suitable bride was secured. She would not meet her husband to be until they stood side by side at the altar, whereat they would be married. This was not unusual in those days, certainly not among royal families.

The Princess arrived for her wedding looking dazzling in a glorious white gown, ornamented with diamonds and white plumes. Her face was veiled. She was surprised, though, not to see crowds thronging the streets. Perhaps the people were republicans? Or perhaps everyone was crammed into the cathedral? But the cathedral was empty too and her footsteps echoed through the high-vaulted walls and arches. At the altar was a bishop, and next to him, the Lindworm.

The Princess was terrified at the sight of him. Do you think she turned tail and fled? Do you think she ran screaming from the cathedral? It would've been better if she had. But, poor woman, she had been brought up to do her duty. Her own mother had told her that her wedding day would be the worst day of her life and after that, it would get harder, and so this poor young woman said, 'Yes' when the bishop asked if she would take this Lindworm to be her ... She and the Lindworm were pronounced Monster and Wife.

But a marriage is not a marriage until the bride and groom have spent the night together. Two guards led the Princess up the stone stairs to the top of the tallest and remotest tower in the King's castle. The poor Princess! Her legs had turned to water, their muscles liquefied by sheer terror. The guards opened the door, pushed her inside, closed the door and made themselves scarce, fast. The Princess couldn't see the room through her tears. But the Lindworm could see her. Lying on a couch (and on the floor and at least once round the room, he was so long), he sat up. He extended one claw towards her, and beckoned, '*Come to be-e-e-ed!*' he hissed. The Princess screamed and tried to open the door to get out. The Lindworm, highly offended, slid swiftly across the room and ate her.

This presented the King and his advisors with a difficulty. First, they had to lie, to tell the parents of the Princess that their daughter had never arrived, and next they had to find a replacement. They did, and she was shown into the same room. '*Come to be-e-e-ed!*' the Lindworm hissed. This time, the Princess fell into a dead faint. She was deader than that in a second, because the Lindworm ate her all up.

Now, this was all proving rather expensive. You can't have princesses disappearing without political repercussions. The advisors suggested to the King that they try the daughters of aristocrats. It was a break with all protocol, not marrying royal to royal, but these were extraordinary circumstances. So lords, dukes, earls and counts were asked if they would like to be united, through their daughters, to the Royal Family. But aristocrats are very clever, especially at keeping what is theirs. Kings come and go but aristocrats remain, quietly owning stuff. They'd heard rumours of princesses disappearing and didn't want their daughters to follow suit, so they blushed at the honour, truly not worthy, couldn't possibly accept, what an honour, and managed to save face and save their daughters' lives. The Lindworm was still wife-less. Then the advisors said something to the King that even shocked themselves. They said, 'Your Majesty, in these extraordinary circumstances, and even though it breaks with all tradition, runs roughshod over all convention and deals with decorum as a dog destroys paper to get at meat,' they would have to secure, for the Lindworm, a commoner to be his bride. The King accepted the idea, more easily than they did. A young woman of common birth was found. But there was nothing common about this common girl.

She was tall and slender, strong and graceful. She was quick-witted and clever, very clever. She was kind and wise beyond her years. She was honest and considerate, truth-telling and truth-dealing. She was witty, loud of laughter, quick to smile, happy to help, glad to give. She sang, she cooked, she helped her father run his little farm, helped her mother with the small children, helped everyone she knew who needed help. Offered the chance to marry a prince, she jumped at it! Her mother and father had always worked so hard, and if she could do something for them to make their old age easier, she would. But she wasn't stupid. She thought something funny must be going on if the King and Queen needed a girl like her to marry their son, so she knew she needed some good advice. Can you guess who she went to for that advice?

The Wise Woman! The Wise Woman had learned something of what had been going on in the palace, and she was glad the Young Woman had come to her. She said, 'I've got a simple question for you. Your wedding day - would you rather be stylish or dead? And on your wedding night, be beautiful or live?'

The Young Woman answered straightaway that she would rather live, and that she thought it a funny question.

'You'd be surprised ...' said the Wise Woman, 'So, you're going to go to your wedding in a dress made of nine layers of cloth and you are going to take with you nine buckets filled with quicklime and nine brushes with strong bristles. Can you do that?'

The Young Woman said she could and so the Wise Woman told her what to do with them.

The very next week, the Young Woman waddled to the cathedral, her body completely buried in a dress made of nine layers of fabric. Entering the cathedral, she looked intently at the Lindworm. He was huge, all scales, spikes, spines, teeth and claws. He was also getting impatient – he'd done this a number of times by now. The bishop said, 'Do you, Lindworm, take this woman to be your ...' and the Lindworm interrupted! '*Yessss I doooo!*' he hissed, '*Get on with it!*'

After the ceremony was concluded the guards came to take the Young Woman by her arms and lead her up the stairs to the chamber where her husband waited for her. They expected to half-carry her – it's what they'd done before. But she shook off their arms and walked confidently up the stairs, asking only that they help her carry the buckets and scrubbing brushes. They were astonished. When they got to the door, *she* opened it. She walked inside. She told the guards where to put the buckets and brushes and then, smiling beautifully, she thanked them and told them they could go now. The guards were stunned! The Young Woman turned and looked at the room. In the top left-hand corner of the room the Lindworm lay on a couch, his head propped up on one of his clawed hands. She saw a movement at the opposite side of the room. It was the Lindworm's tail, twitching. He extended his other claw and beckoned to her; '*Come to be-e-e-e-e-eddd!!*' he hissed.

'Of course. But don't you want me to take my dress off first?' she asked, and the Lindworm nearly fell off his couch in astonishment.

'*Ye-e-e-sssss!*' he hissed, '*Take it offfff!*'

So she took off the first of the nine layers of her dress. This done, she pointed at the Lindworm, 'Your turn!' she said.

The Lindworm looked momentarily nonplussed, but then he dug his sharp claws into the crown of his head, and pulled. There was a ripping sound as he pulled off one entire layer of his skin.

Now, have you seen the way that snakes can shed a layer of skin, leaving behind a perfect cast of a snake? It was like that. The Lindworm pulled off a layer of skin, threw it aside, and there he was, just as large, just as scary, but glistening slightly.

'*Come to be-e-e-eddd!*' he hissed.

'But I'm not undressed yet!' said the Young Woman, and pulled off another layer of her dress, and then, 'Your turn!' So the Lindworm pulled off another layer of skin, and so it went on, she taking off a layer of dress, him taking off a layer of skin, until she was down to only one layer. One thin layer of fabric between her and those claws, those teeth.

'Come to be-e-e-edddddd!!' the Lindworm hissed.

'In a moment!' she said. She took off the last layer of her dress and now stood there in just her skin. Her soft skin. 'Your turn!' she said, and for the first time her voice betrayed her – it faltered, just a little. The Lindworm reached claws to the top of his head and again he pulled, again he ripped. Only, this time, something different happened. He pulled, and there was a great *woop-woop* wobbly noise. Suddenly, instead of a great long Lindworm, that last layer, removed, revealed a large round ball of very thin skin, kind of like an exercise ball or like a huge, free-standing blister. The Young Woman lost no time. She grabbed a bucket, dipped a brush in it and scrubbed.

She scrubbed until her arms were aching, but she didn't stop. She scrubbed until there wasn't a drop of quicklime left in that bucket nor a single bristle left on that brush. She threw them both away and began with the next. This went on, and on, and on and on some more until she was down to the last few drops of quicklime in the last bucket and the last few bristles on the last brush. She was exhausted, but, she told herself, she'd scrubbed pots and floors since she was a child, and this was the same, and there was something else; because she'd scrubbed so much that the skin of this vast blister had got thinner and thinner, so thin that she could see through it, and she could see there was something inside. She couldn't see what it was, but it was definitely something.

Suddenly, the blister burst. There was clear liquid all over the floor and, lying on the floor, staring blindly at the ceiling, there was ... well, what do you think?

Did you think it was the princesses who had been eaten? It was not. It was a young man, in his skin just as she was. She touched his skin and it was cold.

There was a bed at the other side of the room and so the young woman took hold of the young man's wrist and pulled his arm up and over her shoulders. She helped him to stand, and he needed her help because his legs were all bent up after being inside that blister for so long. She helped him limp and stagger towards the bed. She dropped him on one side, pulled the heavy covers over him, then she got in the other side. She held him tight, that she might warm him with her warmth. All through that night, his body would jerk and spasm, and he gave little cries. She held him, and stroked his head soothingly. It was only as the early light was filtering through the shutters that he spoke words.

'It was awful!' he said, still staring at something a thousand miles away.

'It's alright,' she said, 'it's over now.'

'You have no idea what it was like!' he gasped, 'Doing those things! Unable to stop myself, just being so very, very angry!'

'It's alright,' she said, 'I'm here now.'

And he turned and looked at her. For the first time, their eyes met. So she kissed him.

In the morning, to everyone's astonishment, the door of that high-towered room opened. The Young Woman stepped out and with her came a very shy young man. This oldest son now met his father, who welcomed him, and his mother, who begged, begged his forgiveness. He embraced her and said he was glad to be alive. He met his younger brother, who said, a little awkwardly, that now there was an oldest son he couldn't be king one day but at least he could get married now. There was a princess he'd been corresponding with for some time, and he'd really like to ... The oldest son said to him, 'My brother, all your life you have been raised to be a king and you will be a fine king. I have seen too much of action already, stuck inside that monstrous body! I will be your loyal subject and, for myself, want nothing more now than a quiet life, with my wife.'

So it was done. The King and Queen embraced their older son. The youngest son went haring off on the fastest horse he could find to fling himself at the feet of the girl he'd fallen in love with and the oldest son and his wife moved to a lovely house in a gorgeous part of the country where they lived happily, growing vegetables, keeping chickens and sheep, and raising a large and noisy family in the peace of that quiet valley. And you know what? Not one of their children was born a Lindworm!

☞ 'The Lindworm' and 'Thorn Rose' – Structural Investigation and Comparison

So I gave you 'The Lindworm' as an example of the Form of Story known as Rebirth. You may have noticed how similar, in bones form, it is to 'Snow White'? Look at the way that the childlessness of one generation leads to action that leads to an imperfect solution, which is only made perfect when a second-generation character is Reborn. Snow White coughs up the apple and rises from the casket, the Lindworm sheds his skin and releases the Prince. But you may have also felt that there were elements in this story that reminded you of the Quest? You're right - three Quests actually.

You are about to get a sneak preview of a subject we'll come back to in Four Types of Plot. We will go through this quickly now and in detail later. For now, it's enough that you just notice how the Queen's story is a Quest that goes partially wrong and gets stuck at her Stage 5 (Enemy/Obstacle) - one of her children comes out wrong because she did not succeed in following the Wise Woman's instructions. At this point the focus of the story shifts - the Queen is no longer the main subject of the narrative; one of her two sons is, the princely one. We learn that he is on a Quest of his own and in summary form we go through five stages:

1. Who and Where - the Prince.
2. Problem - he wishes to get married.
3. Journey - he discusses his wishes with his father.
4. Friend - his father has already made enquiries and the Prince is helped on his Journey towards marriage until ...
5. He meets a massive scaly monster, a Lindworm, who blocks his way.

The Prince's story, like the Queen's, is now stuck at Stage 5. Different attempts are made to solve Stage 5, to marry the Lindworm and thereby free the Prince to go to Stage 6, but because the Lindworm keeps eating the princesses the whole story is now stuck in a recurrent loop. Until a new Quest opens, that of the Young Woman. Her story, told very briefly, is nonetheless a complete Quest:

1. Who and Where - Young Woman, not a princess, intelligent and brave, selected for the Lindworm.
2. Problem - she has to find a solution to the problem of marrying a monster.
3. Journey - she goes looking for advice.
4. Friend/Help - the Wise Woman, who gives her advice and also tools in the form of a nine-layered dress, nine metal buckets of lime and nine scrubbing brushes.
5. Enemy/Obstacle - the Lindworm - big, scary, fierce, angry. As she sheds dresses he sheds skin but doesn't get any less scary.
6. Resolution - last skin shed, Prince released, the Young Woman escapes being eaten.

The clever thing about this story (Scandinavian in origin) is the way that the Stage 6 Resolution for the Young Woman simultaneously allows the Prince to pass Stage 5 in his story and move to his Stage 6, where he gets married and also releases the Queen from her Stage 5, one child coming out wrong, and allows her to move to the Resolution of her original Quest, to have a child, except she now has two. Fair play - she's probably been stuck at Stage 5 for roughly twenty years. Looked at from the focal point of the Queen, the Prince and Young Woman, these stories are all Quests.

But the story is called 'The Lindworm'. Looked at from the point of view of the Lindworm himself, the structure goes:

1. Who, Where and in What Positive Condition? - children are conceived by means of the Queen eating fruit.
2. Negative Agent of Change - the Queen doesn't peel the one fruit as instructed and so one child is born inside a monstrous skin.
3. Submersion of Protagonist - one child is trapped inside a monster, feeling monstrous rage. He is exiled from his family, from humankind and cannot find release until ...
4. Positive Agent of Change - the Young Woman goes to the Wise Woman and, unlike the Queen, follows the advice given.
5. Rebirth - the Lindworm Prince is freed and assumes his true identity.

So 'The Lindworm' is a Rebirth story with a series of Quests nested inside it. For a moment, can you take this chance to think how you may be able to do this in the story of 'Thorn Rose'? How, for example, you might shift the focus of your storytelling to each of the princes who come to rescue her? Why? Who are they and what are they hoping for? What makes the last prince different? I'm not suggesting you must do this but I simply wanted to draw your attention to the fact that you can. We shall return to the subject of Nested Narrative later under Four Types of Plot. For now, read on ...

5

Comedy

If you felt Rebirth was a little solemn, would now be a good time to introduce a lighter note as we explore the next Form of Story, Comedy?

The structure of Comedy in Europe was first analysed by the playwrights in ancient Athens in the fifth century BC. If you read the work of Aristophanes today and you know a little of Athenian current affairs 2,500 years ago, or if you see a cleverly staged modern production, it is very easy to find yourself howling with laughter, wiping tears from your eyes, because of jokes that were first cracked twenty-five centuries ago. But did you know that, simply because something is a Comedy it doesn't *have* to be funny? No, and if you've ever seen a production of Shakespeare's *All's Well that Ends Well*, you might well have asked yourself why that play is classed as one of Shakespeare's Comedies? But, formally, it is not essential that a Comedy make its audience laugh, far from it. The crucial thing about Comedy is that it starts in a world that is in balance, everything in its proper place and order and then imbalance, starting comparatively small, leads to further imbalance until eventually the whole order of things is at risk of complete collapse. This imbalance should reach a point of genuine danger before the action begins to climb out of chaos and order is restored. This return to order is often as accidental as the original descent into chaos/disorder. In Tragedy (which we'll come to shortly), things end badly and order is restored by a purgation that usually means lots of death; in Comedy, everything comes right in the end without the bloodletting. Or, to put it another way, all's well that ends well. Not that you need them, but some examples of this form include *Twelfth Night*, *Being There*, *A Fish Called Wanda*, *Some Like it Hot*, *The Importance of Being Earnest* and *Four Lions*.

So, now you know you are under no pressure to be funny, shall we have a go at creating your first story using the comedic structure? You know the score by now. Please create an image (and this is an *easy* one!) at the entrance to your Memory Palace that will make you remember the word 'Comedy'. Let's start with a really stripped-down structure:

1. Who, Where and What status quo.
2. Imbalance (lads chatting in a car are actually extremists, Olivia won't marry Orsino - i.e. the man whom, conventionally, she should marry - Chance the Gardener, a simpleton, is believed to be a genius, two male musicians have to dress as women in order to get work).
3. Imbalance leads to misunderstanding. Actions based on misunderstanding lead to deeper imbalance, further misguided action, further imbalance. Repeat this bit as often as you like.
4. As a consequence of misunderstandings, real risk is introduced.
5. Risk intensifies.
6. Point of danger reached.
7. Danger passed. Order re-established, perhaps by a figure of authority? Seniority? Accident? Status quo is restored.

Example Story – 'Lazy Jack'

This story is an absolute favourite with schoolchildren from 4 to 11 and I have often told it to entire primary schools at morning assembly to start a school visit. It's worth noting, though, that I have also told it to executives of a huge multinational company who had asked me for a story on the theme of 'context'. In recent years an author has taken this traditional story and turned it into a picture book and the result is that children all over England now already know the story and I have to choose something different. I believe the correct expression is 'sassen, frassan, rassen ...'?

Years and years ago, in England, there lived a woman and her son, whose name was Jack. They weren't rich, far from it! They lived in a small cottage on a patch of ground on which Jack's mother grew all the food they ate. Jack's mother had to work very hard. If her vegetables grew well that was good, because then they had enough to eat. When her vegetables grew better than well, that was better, but they didn't eat any better. Why? Because Jack's mother didn't own the land on which they lived. All the land around was owned by one man, the Squire, and every year, the Squire would send his men for the rent. So all year round, Jack's mother saved hard! Whenever she harvested more food than they needed to eat she took the surplus to the market, sold it, and when she got the money, she brought it home and popped it in a box. She never treated Jack, let alone herself, to anything nice. She knew that, if she ever failed to save enough money to pay the rent, then the Squire would send other men, nasty men, who would turn Jack and his mother out of their cottage. They would have to beg in the streets and sleep in the hedgerows and before the sun had set another family would be living in their little house.

Now, while she worked so hard, do you think Jack helped her? He did not. If it was a nice sunny day, Jack would stretch out in front of the cottage and enjoy the warmth of the sun. If it was a cold day, Jack would stretch out in front of the fire (which his mother had made) and enjoy the warmth of the fire. This is why people in the area said he was lazy, and in fact, that's what they called him – Lazy Jack.

But one day Lazy Jack's mother came to him in distress. She'd counted the money she'd saved that year, and there wasn't enough to pay the rent! In seven days time the Squire's men would be coming for the rent and she didn't have enough money! Frowning, her eyes wild with anxiety, she told Jack, and Jack said, 'Whatever ...'

'Don't you "Whatever" me, young man!' his mother snapped. 'If we don't have enough money by the end of the week you won't have a cottage to lie in front of if it's warm, nor a fire to lie by if it's not!'

Even Jack could see that this was serious. His mother told him that, the next day, he had to walk to town, to the market, and there find a stall called the Hiring Stall. The Hiring Stall was like a Job Centre; if you needed work you went and stood there and if someone needed someone to work for them they might hire you.

So, the next day, Jack walked to the town. He found the market, and the Hiring Stall, and stood there hoping someone would hire him. His mother had told him to work hard and then, when he got paid, to bring the money home to her.

I don't know if you'd have thought that Jack looked like the man for the job, or for any job, but somebody did, because he was hired by a carpenter. As you know, carpenters are very skilled at shaping wood and making wood into tables, and chairs, and desks, and cupboards and many other things that people need. This carpenter had an order for lots of chairs and he hired Jack simply to carry planks of timber to him as he worked at his carpenter's bench, so he could just keep making and wouldn't lose any time in fetching and carrying. So Jack spent all day carrying planks of oak, of pine, of walnut, of cherry, whatever the carpenter needed for whatever he was making.

Actually, Jack enjoyed it! He'd never known a day go by so fast. At the end of the day the carpenter said to him, 'Thank you Jack, I like the way you've worked for me! I don't need you tomorrow, so I'll pay you now.'

He reached into his leather purse and gave Jack a large, shiny silver coin.

Jack was so thrilled! Have you ever been paid money for doing a job of work? And if you have, can you remember the first time, and how proud you felt, and how that money felt really *yours*? Well, Jack knew the money had to go to his mother, but nonetheless, as he looked at that coin, he thought it the loveliest thing he'd ever seen in his life. He tilted it in his hand and gasped when he saw the light flashing from it in different directions. So he balanced it on his thumb and forefinger and flipped it into the air, then caught it. This was even lovelier, because, as that coin tumbled and fell, the light went flashing in all directions.

So, as he walked through the streets, it was flip! And catch.

As he walked through the fields it was flip! And catch.

As he walked through the woods it was flip! And catch.

And as he walked over the bridge where the river ran fast and deep it was flip! And ...

'Oh no!'

You can guess where that coin went, can't you? It landed in the river, the river grabbed it and swept it away and that was the last Jack ever saw of that coin.

When he got home, his mother said, 'Did you work for me today, Jack?'

'Yes Mum.'

'Did you get paid?'

'Yes Mum.'

'Can I have the money then?'

And Jack told her that she could not. When he told her why, she was so angry. She shrieked at him, 'You are a very *stupid* young man!'

'Yes Mum, sorry Mum.'

'You should've put it in your pocket!'

'Yes Mum, sorry Mum.'

'Go out and work for me tomorrow and, when you get paid, put it in your pocket!'

'Yes Mum, sorry Mum.'

So Jack went out to work the next day, and on this day he was hired by a farmer. Now, this farmer had much more land than Jack and his mother did, and he kept a herd of cows for their milk. Some of his staff were sick so he had to do all the milking himself and he hired Jack to drive the cows into the milking parlour. Jack loved this work; it was amazing! These huge animals, great boulders of meat and muscle, would lumber forwards when he raised his arm and shouted, 'Go on there!'

And, once they were inside the dairy, the farmer milked them and all the milk was collected in a huge tank.

At the end of the day, the dairy farmer said, 'Thank you Jack, I like the way you've worked for me today. Now, I'd love to pay you money but I'm saving money for the Squire's men. How're you getting on with that?'

Jack ducked his head from side to side, mumbled nothing in particular.

'That's good!' said the farmer, 'Now, I can't give you money but I can give you something your mother will be happy with. I can give you the best milk in the world, fresh out of the cow!'

And, with that, he took a large brown jug, dipped it in the tank and, when he brought it out, it was full to the brim with fresh milk. He gave the jug to Jack.

Now, can you remember what Jack's mother said he should do when he got paid? That's right! He should put it in his pocket. Jack tried to put the large brown jug in his pocket, but, try as he might, he couldn't make it fit. So, he opened his pocket with his other hand, and ...

Glug!

Glug!

Glug!

He poured all that milk into his pocket. It ran down his leg. It got into his socks and made cheese between his toes. It got into his underpants, and everything squelched as he walked, uncomfortably, home.

When he got home, his mother hit the roof. 'You are a very *stupid* young man!'

'Yes Mum, sorry Mum!'

'You should've carried it on your head!'

'Yes Mum, sorry Mum.'

'Next time you go out and work for me, when you get paid, carry it on your head, do you understand?'

'Yes Mum, sorry Mum.'

'Just remember, carry it on your head!'

So, the next day, Jack went out to work and he was hired by the same dairy farmer. So it's looking OK so far, isn't it? Again, he worked very hard. Again, he'd never known a day go by so fast nor seem so full, and full of interest, and, at the end of the day, the dairy farmer said to him, 'How did that milk go down, did that milk go down alright?'

Jack said that it had, and shook his leg uncomfortably.

'Well, I won't give you milk again, but I've got something really special for you this time ...'

Turning round, he selected for Jack a really big soft cheese, as big as a plate and shaped to sit on one. So, can you remember what Jack's mother said he should do when he got paid?

That's right! Carry it on his head. So Jack did, and that's not such a bad idea, there are lots of people who carry things on their head. You can take a lot of weight on your head and it leaves your hands free for other things. So Jack balanced the large flat, round cheese on this head and began the walk home.

Unfortunately, it was a hot, sunny day and as Jack walked the cheese began to soften. It began to sag, it began to bubble, it began to dribble, it began to melt all over Jack's head. By the time he got home, Jack couldn't see which way we was going. He was wearing a helmet made out of cheese and there was only one tiny little hole that he could see through (if he'd have been a character in *Star Wars* they'd have to call him Darth Cheddar).

And when he got home his mother exploded, 'You are a very *stuupiid* young man!'

'Yes Mum, sorry Mum.'

'You should've carried it in your two hands in front of you! And if it got hot, you should've dipped it in the water!'

'Yes Mum, sorry Mum.'

'For goodness sake Jack, we need the money! So, when you get paid tomorrow, carry it in your two hands in front of you and, if it gets hot, dip it in the water!'

'Yes Mum. Sorry Mum.'

So the next day, when Jack went out to work, he was hired by a miller. The miller was a very important man who had the job of grinding lots of grain, be it wheat, or barley, or oats, or rye, or millet, or buckwheat into flour so that people could make bread. Now, can you guess what, of all things in the world, the miller was most afraid of? He was frightened of something getting into his grain store and eating his grains before he could grind them into flour, sell that flour and turn it into money. Can you think what it is that would eat the grains?

That's right; the miller was frightened of mice! Without him seeing them, he knew that mice could eat their way through his grain store and leave him much poorer. So his mill was crawling with cats. Now these weren't nice cats that you could pet and fuss, these cats were there for one reason and one reason only. These cats were there to kill mice. The miller didn't feed them. If they were hungry they'd do a better job and they would catch and kill more mice. Jack was nervous of these cats that prowled around as he carried sack after sack of wheat, of barley, of oats. They looked at him like he was nothing.

At the end of the day the miller said, 'Thank you Jack, I like the way you've worked for me! Now, I can't afford to give you money 'cos I've got none until I sell this next load of flour, but I can give you something your mother will be glad of. Now, haven't you got mice on your little field?'

Jack ducked his head from side to side, mumbled nothing in particular.

'That's right Jack, of course you have! Now, to help you and your mum keep the mice down I'm going to give you, as payment, one of my best mouse-killing cats.'

The miller went off. Jack winced when he heard a commotion, some hissing and yowling, and then saw the miller coming back, carrying a cat. Now, you know the right way to carry a cat, don't you? You put one hand under its ribs with its front legs separated by your fingers. Your other hand cups under the cat's back legs, and that way the cat doesn't feel scared and it doesn't hurt the cat because the weight of its back legs isn't stretching their spine. Now, Jack was looking at this cat uncertainly, because one of its ears was torn to shreds from fights. One of its eyes was missing from fights. There were scars all over its face from fights.

'Nice puss,' said Jack, unconvincingly, 'is it called Tiddles? Or Pansy?'

'No,' said the miller, and here he handed the cat to Jack, 'He's called the Terminator!'

Now Jack was really scared, and the cat was growling a low growl. And do you remember what Jack's mother said he should do when he got paid?

So Jack took the cat and carried it in his two hands, holding it at arms' length while its back legs, which hung down, unsupported, did their best to kick out, hoping to disembowel Jack if they could only reach. As Jack walked down the road the cat yowled and growled. As Jack continued, the cat began to hiss and spit, and all the while, narrowed and burning with murderous intent, glowed its remaining eye.

Now Jack was very scared and he was trying, desperately, to think. He listened to the hissing sound the cat was making and he thought that reminded him of something. When his mother was cooking, sometimes her pots would make a similar sound and Jack's mum would take them off the heat, because that sound meant they were too hot. So, can you remember what Jack's mother said he should do if it got hot?

How fortunate for Jack that he happened to be passing the pond. He walked to the edge of the pond, bent down, and dipped the cat in the water, just as you might dip a biscuit into your tea. The cat went absolutely berserk, hissing, howling, scratching, slashing. It scratched Jack down both his arms. It scratched Jack across his chest. It scratched Jack across his face. Jack shrieked and let go of the cat, which ran out of sight (and out of this story).

When Jack got home, cut and bleeding, his mother erupted! She screamed at him, 'You are a very *stuuupppiiid* young man!'

'Yes Mum, sorry Mum.'

'You should've tied a string around it and pulled it behind you down the street!'

'Yes Mum, sorry Mum.'

'Go out and work for me tomorrow, Jack, and please! When you get paid, tie a string round it and pull it behind you down the street!'

And then Jack's mum felt bad, because she didn't like to shout at her son, but really! They only had two more days to make some money and then the Squire's men would be coming and, the way things stood now, they would have no home and they would have to beg in the streets and sleep in the hedgerows, and that wasn't a life she wanted for herself or her son.

So the next day Jack went out to work and he was hired by a butcher. Now, you know what a butcher sells, don't you? Jack and his mum didn't get to eat meat very often, no more than two or three times a year, but, even so, Jack knew what a butcher sold and I'm sure you do too. So all of that day Jack worked hard, carrying sides of beef, of lamb, of pork, so the butcher could chop them into cuts, cut them into chops, mince them into mince and stuff them into sausages. At the end of the day the butcher said, 'Thank you Jack, I like the way you've worked for me! Now, I could give you money but I can be much more generous if I pay you in kind, does that make sense? So how about I give you this lovely big leg of lamb?'

Now Jack remembered he'd tasted leg of lamb once and that ever after he'd wanted to taste it again, so he was happy to accept. The butcher chose a really lovely big leg of lamb and gave it to Jack.

And can you guess what Jack did with it? That's right! He tied a string round it and dragged it behind him down the street.

Now, is that any way to treat food you mean to eat? He hadn't got far before the meat was mucky and dirty and messy, so much so that it would put you off your food. But it didn't put the dogs off. As soon as they smelled meat being dragged through the street they ran and grabbed at it with their teeth. Jack tried to shoo them away but there were just too many of them! And when the dogs had done their work, it was the cats' turn. And after the cats came the rats, then the mice, then the beetles, then the woodlice, then the ants, then ... and then ... and then ... When Jack got home and his mother asked him, 'Did you work for me today?'

He said, 'Yes Mum.'

'And did you get paid today?'

'Yes Mum.'

'And can I have the money then?'

Jack whisked his hand from behind him and held up to his mother ... can you guess?

A bone.

A bone picked so clean of meat that it could've come from the Natural History Museum. Jack's mother was apoplectic, 'You are a very *stttuuuuuupppppiiiiiid* young man!'

To which Jack said, 'Mother, I confess that, as this discourse has progressed I have, resultantly, been formulating a new and adapted self-concept, the better to approach convergence criteria with the view which you yourself have heretofore so vehemently predicated.'

Jack's mother stopped, blinked and swallowed like an owl, and then, 'What was that?'

'I don't know Mum.'

'Where did it come from?'

'I don't know Mum.'

'What does it mean?'

'I don't know Mum.'

'What did you say it for then?'

'I don't know Mum.'

'*You are a very stuuuuuuuuuupppppiiiiid young man!*'

'Yes Mum. Sorry Mum.'

'You should've carried it on your shoulder Jack! Jack, it's the last day tomorrow! Please, please, please, when you get paid, carry it on your shoulder!'

So on the last day Jack went out to work and he was hired by a farmer. This farmer only had a little bit of land, but it was bigger than that which Jack and his mother had. Jack worked hard all day for that farmer and for the first time he really understood how hard his mother had been working all these years. He thought to himself, 'If we get through this, I will help Mum much more.'

At the end of the day the farmer said to Jack, 'Thank you Jack, I like the way you've worked for me today. Now, I don't need you tomorrow so I should pay you now. Trouble is, I can't pay you cash. I'm saving money for the Squire's men ...'

Jack nodded.

'How're you and your mum getting on with that?'

'Oh, you know,' said Jack, in a way that said nothing.

'Good, good!' said the farmer. 'Listen! I have to buy a new donkey, because my old donkey, Eric, he's getting too old now to work my land. I can't afford to feed two donkeys but Eric's a good old sort, a friend, so I don't want to just hit him on the head with a hammer. So, as payment, I'd like to give you my donkey, Eric. He'll be useful to you both on your little bit of land for a good few years yet!'

Jack said thank you. Jack and Eric the Donkey were introduced. Now, can you remember what Jack's mother said he should do when he got paid?

Personally, I can't imagine how he did it, but somehow Jack managed to get a whole donkey up on his shoulder, and began to carry it home. The donkey was braying and its legs were kicking in the air. The donkey was so heavy that Jack took a short cut through the town. At a certain point, the donkey slipped and Jack only just caught it before it touched the ground, but now the donkey's front legs were going over Jack's shoulders and the donkey's back legs were going round Jack's waist. Jack couldn't see where he was going and he couldn't walk straight. It looked, for all the world, like Jack and the donkey were dancing together.

As Jack staggered through town a crowd of people gathered, pointing and laughing, 'Look at the funny man dancing with the donkey!'

Because Jack couldn't see which way he was going, he accidentally went through the rich part of town, and he even went past the house of the richest man in the town, the mayor. Now this mayor, for all that he was powerful and rich, was a sad man. Years ago, his wife had died, leaving him and their baby daughter behind her. This little girl had been so sad after her mummy died that she had never spoken a word nor laughed since. She had grown up into an intelligent, kind and thoughtful young woman, but she was totally silent!

The rich man had brought doctors. They couldn't do anything, but thought that, maybe, if someone could make her laugh that might get her talking again? The rich man had hired clowns. That didn't work. He hired comedians. That didn't work. He was so desperate he even hired storytellers, and of course that didn't work! Some years ago he had, in distress, put an advert in the newspaper saying that any young man who could make his daughter laugh and restore her power of speech would be rewarded with her hand in marriage and, when the rich man retired, they would inherit all his connections and be rich and powerful. So, of course, lots of young men came to try and make her laugh. Do you think they succeeded?

They did not! None of them were funny, at least not to her, and many of them weren't even young. She just sat there, sad and silent, while they cracked all their favourite jokes. The rich man's daughter stayed silent and single.

Now, the rich man was at his desk that day, looking at a spreadsheet. In the background he could just hear the faint sound of a donkey. Then he heard the most amazing sound, 'Hee hee hee! Daddy, look at the funny man dancing with the donkey!'

Who do you think said that? The rich man looked up, amazed, 'Darling, you just laughed!'

'Yes Daddy, I did!'

'And you spoke!'

'Yes Daddy, I did!'

'And you're speaking now! You're cured!'

The rich man looked out and saw Jack with the donkey.

'That's the man!' he cried. He grabbed his daughter by the wrist and rushed for the door. She was still laughing when they got outside. The rich man ran up to Jack and said, 'You, sir, put down that donkey and meet your wife!'

Jack put down the donkey, looked up, and practically fell into the loveliest eyes he had ever seen in his life. He blushed and looked at the floor. The rich man's daughter felt something very deeply when she came face to face with Jack, and she blushed and looked at the floor.

Even the donkey blushed and looked at the floor.

Now, the rich man was a very decisive man, so he took Jack and his daughter to a chapel and they were married within the hour. He gave away his daughter's hand in marriage. The donkey was Jack's best man and made a better best man's speech than some I've heard.

That night, Jack's mother was in her little cottage tearing her hair out with worry. Where was her son? Had he been paid? Would this little home be their home tomorrow? Or somebody else's? Suddenly she looked up and saw her son with a silly grin on his face and a pretty girl by his side.

'Did you work for me today Jack?' she asked.

'Yes Mum, I did.'

'Did you get paid today?'

'Yes Mum, I did.'

'Can I have the money then?'

'Not exactly ...'

'What do you mean 'not exactly'?' she gasped.

'Mum, this is my wife!' said Jack, all in a rush.

'*Wife!*' shrieked his mum, 'we can't afford a wife!'

'And Mum, this is my father-in-law!'

At this, the richest man in the town stepped into their little hut. He was smiling and he had his arms out.

'My lady,' he said, 'I can promise you, you will never need to worry about money ever again, because you and I are family now, connected through the love of our children!'

Well, Jack's mother was so relieved she burst into tears.

So Jack, his wife, the rich man and Jack's mother all lived happily together until the end of their days. I don't know if it was at that first meeting that Jack's mother and the rich man realised they liked each other, but the two of them were very happy together. And as for Jack and his wife? They were very happy together!

And do you think that was the last time Jack's wife laughed *at* her husband, or do you think she laughed at him again?

She laughed at him many times, joyously, but Jack didn't mind. Jack didn't mind because the laughter was always kind and, fool that he was (and he was, she told him!), Jack was at least wise enough to know that, when a woman laughs at her man, that can be taken as evidence that she loves him.

Comedy Advanced

In 2017 I was hired by Shakespeare's Globe Theatre in Southwark, London, to run a storymaking session with a group of children who didn't know each other and at least some of them were visually impaired. It was part of their Telling Tales Festival. I looked more closely at the structure of Shakespeare's Comedies and drew up the following worksheet, from which we were able to create and retell, in just one hour, a functional story that was genuinely funny. The seed of the structure featured characters with poor self-awareness and the Action of the story serves to bring them, through chaos, accident, mistake and mischance, to a more accurate view of themselves. See what you can do with the following:

1. Character Who and Where - someone important, admirable:
    - 1.1. High Self-Belief - what do they think of themselves?
    - 1.2. But in fact ... keep this unstated - let actions show it.
2. Character Opposite - Who and Where:
    - 1.1. High Self-Belief - what do they think of themselves?
    - 1.2. But in fact ... again, let Action disclose this.
    - 1.2.1. Sub-plot Who and Where - a caricature of 1.1.
    - 1.2.2. Sub-plot Opposite Who and Where - a caricature of 2.1.
3. Newcomer - Who and Where - a version of who 1.1 could be/should be.
4. Newcomer Opposite - Who and Where - a version of who 2.1 could be/should be.
5. Imbalances - first, suggest how things should be? Then show characters attaching wrongly to the characters:
    - 5.1. Sub-plot - echo/reflect.
6. Misunderstandings:
    - 6.1. Main plot.
    - 6.2. Sub-plot.
7. Complications:
    - 7.1. Main plot.
    - 7.2. Sub-plot.
    - REPEAT.
    - REPEAT.
8. Danger.
9. REVEAL - danger passes.
10. Order restored and Character 1 and 2 come to real self-knowledge.

I know this seems a bit complicated, the reason being that, as we touched on in our structural Investigation of 'The Lindworm' earlier, this is not the story arc of one character but six.

This is where the dramatic begins to really diverge from the epic (from which early drama grew). The story arcs of multiple characters are placed not consecutively, as in 'The Lindworm', but simultaneously and they are interwoven. It's a little hard but only hard, not impossible - try it. At the Globe we managed to create a really good story with this Form of Story that, in true comedic fashion, if I ever did write it down afterwards, I have subsequently lost. I do know it featured a proud young Queen who thought herself a great dancer (I think she was a giraffe) and who declared she would marry the winner of a dance contest, which was entered by a love-struck but cumbersome Rhinoceros with four left feet and a crush on the Queen, who attempted his winning performance on some rotten floorboards with hilarious consequences ... I did not invent *any* of these elements - a group of children, whom I'd never met before and who had never met each other did.

We laughed a lot making this up, our minds set free by following the rules. I would argue that the very specificity of this story structure is what enabled Shakespeare to repeat the success of *The Comedy of Errors* with *The Taming of the Shrew, A Midsummer Night's Dream, Much Ado About Nothing, As You Like It, Twelfth Night, The Merry Wives of Windsor, All's Well that Ends Well* and *Measure for Measure*. If you follow a structure that is *content free*, you can greatly speed up the creation of a new story while at the same time enjoying some confidence that it will work because, structurally, it's been done before. Time not spent on testing a new structure can be spent instead on new invention within that structure.

So, try the above. You may be pleasantly surprised ...

6

Tragedy

Tragedy was the other great cornerstone of Ancient Greek drama, all of which, of course, was the dramatic and scenographic realisation of traditional oral stories. As a form, Tragedy is still much in use today. We learned earlier that all Comedies are not necessarily funny. Now it is important to point out that just because a story has a sad ending does *not* mean it is a Tragedy. A Quest, for example, can end in failure, disaster, death. A real-life example might be 1967 and Donald Campbell's attempt to break the world water speed record in *Bluebird*, which ended so disastrously and so very publicly. It is not a Tragedy, I would argue, because it is not a feature of Campbell's personality that leads to his death but rather a Quest that failed. Similarly, Rags to Riches can end with the test of exalted status *not* being passed successfully and the Rags returned. In the case of the 1960s classic *Bonny and Clyde*, their Rags to Riches escapade ends in their death, yet, I would argue, this is *not* a Tragedy. This is quite apart from the fact that Bonny and Clyde were thoroughly unpleasant people. Formally, their story is not a Tragedy but Rags to Riches. So what does make a Tragedy a Tragedy?

In Tragedy, we witness a reversal of fortune for a person of great quality, great potential and/or great importance. The Tragic protagonist is presented with a Challenge, as in a Quest, but due to a personal quality (the Tragic flaw) of which they themselves have insufficient awareness, they respond to it in ways that intensify, rather than solve this Challenge. The very nature of the Challenge runs straight up against the very nature of the character's Tragic flaw and the Action of the story will expose it. This flaw and the character's failure to deal with it impels the protagonist through events that seem to develop a momentum of their own.

This momentum is known as the 'Tragic Wheel'; once it starts turning, the protagonist can't seem to stop it. With mounting intensity and danger, a series of events befall the protagonist that appear to be, but needn't be inevitable, except that, at each turn, the character fails to overcome their personal weakness and makes the wrong choice. For example, Hamlet is given a very clear command by his father's ghost: avenge my murder, kill your uncle. People other than Hamlet have seen this ghost, so Hamlet needn't fear for his sanity. Should he need them, he has witnesses. It is Hamlet's inability to act, his Tragic flaw, which leads to the deaths of not only his uncle but also his mother, his girlfriend, her father, her brother, two of his college friends and Hamlet himself. If you haven't seen *Hamlet*, I apologise for the spoiler.

The tragedy of *Macbeth* can appear to be the opposite and, superficially, it is. Macbeth's tragedy begins because, unlike Hamlet, who doesn't act when he should, Macbeth does act when he shouldn't. The element of a Challenge mistaken because of a Tragic flaw is the same. Macbeth is swayed by his own and his wife's ambition into committing a crime in order to gain a prize promised him by the witches' prophecy. He himself debates whether he needs to seize this prize or whether he can't simply wait for it to fall to him anyway, as the first boon promised by the witches has. It is his choice, which is based on his personality, that of a man of vigorous and decisive action, which leads to all the blood (and the ticket sales! That's one popular play!).

An ancient Greek example would be the story of Antigone, or of her father Oedipus. If Antigone could only obey the new ruler, King Creon, and value peace higher than piety, everything would be alright. An excellent Victorian example of Tragic story structure would be Oscar Wilde's *The Picture of Dorian Gray*. Blessed with everything, Dorian makes a Tragic choice, prompted by a flaw in his character, vanity. David Cronenberg's film, *The Fly*, is structurally such a superb modern realisation of the Tragic form that it has been turned into an opera.

An even better example than *The Fly*, because its more plausible, is Martin Scorsese's *Mean Streets*, in which Harvey Keitel's character, Charlie, is trying to move up in the local Mob. He is seen to have potential and, as the film progresses, we learn that some in the Mob wish to induct him into the privileged elite of 'made men'. Charlie's Tragic flaw is one of loyalty to and concern for his friend, Johnny Boy, who is played by Robert De Niro. This is a particularly strong Tragic situation because we, as viewers, are torn between our sense of Charlie's loyalty to his friend being a good thing and our sense that Johnny Boy's recklessness and stupidity is going to lead to disaster. We like Charlie for his loyalty but we fear the Mob will be less sympathetic.

Important in this Form is a tension between our belief that the protagonist can and maybe will just about make the right decision and a growing sense of dread that they won't. Once the Tragic Wheel is turning, it is important that it seems to develop its own momentum and there's almost no stopping it, even though we hope against hope that there is. And then, in real life, a good example of Tragedy (and remember, it is my contention that these Forms of Story do reflect the ways in which we process our experiences of real life) might be found in the fall from grace of the cyclist Lance Armstrong. At some point, Armstrong chose to cheat, his Action prompted by his Tragic flaw, ambition. That choice will have led to complication after complication until, eventually, he was caught and stripped of all his trophies, his star falling from glory into ignominy.

Another real-life example, also from sport, might be the story of American heavyweight boxer Tommy Morrison. An exceptionally talented athlete, born in 1969, Morrison held a world title. He enjoyed the perks of his success to the point where he was turning up for fights underprepared, visibly bloated by drink and drugs. A handsome man, he also enjoyed the attentions of women and was, for a time, simultaneously married to two women, both called Dawn. His career saw some very notable highs followed by notable lows and then comeback and further highs. In 1996 he was forced to submit the blood test he had been avoiding and he tested positive for HIV. Scandal followed - how long had he known? How could he put opponents at risk? In 2006 he attempted a comeback, claiming his test result was falsified, and fought two further fights. In 2013 his mother announced his death from complications of AIDS. Honestly, read the Wikipedia page, it's tragic.

It is not essential that we like a Tragic protagonist. For example, I don't like Macbeth. Do you? What is essential is that we identify with a Tragic protagonist's struggle. So, for instance, I've never been tempted by unexpected prophecy to murder my friend and benefactor in order to replace him, as Macbeth is, but I do have experience of ambition and of the great difficulties associated with achieving my ambitions. Have I ever felt that somebody is occupying a place that I would like to fill? Yes. So, although I have never (yet) felt tempted to murder someone to achieve my ambitions, I can identify with Macbeth's struggle. I can certainly identify with Hamlet, faced so young with a demand on him to which he doesn't feel he can rise. Who can't remember late adolescence and the need to make important life decisions with a minimum of actual life experience? And who has not, like Charlie in *Mean Streets*, ever chosen to support a friend or maintain a connection more out of loyalty than good judgement? Tragedy is all around us.

You might wonder if this form is appropriate for a child? Well, it's your child and it's your call, but I quote the Kiowa Apache storyteller Dovie Thomason, who, when asked about the wisdom of telling hard-hitting stories to children, said, 'There's no child worth so little they don't deserve to be told how hard life can be.' I refer you to the earlier section on the psychological benefits of exposure to scary stories. When I tell hard-hitting stories to children, and I do, it is a judgement call and it is also a matter of degree. So, in 'Orange, Lemon and Lime' , I do say that Mummy cut Orange's throat. I do *not* say that the blood came bubbling and hissing from the deep slash, spreading like a scarlet smile across Orange's neck, nor do I mention the smell of fresh blood, nor rub their noses in it. You can tell children a Tragic story but you don't have to put them in it, or through it.

At some point, all children learn that all life ends. It's odd; I can't remember learning this. I can remember learning to ride a bike. I can remember learning to whistle, but I can't remember learning that one day I and everyone I know will die. Better that a child learn this from a story than an air raid, surely? A good example of a story that many children love and which has Tragic elements would be Hans Christian Andersen's 'The Little Mermaid'. She gains legs but loses her prince and feels agony with every step she takes. For a free-swimming mermaid, I reckon that constitutes a reversal of fortune. Tragedy is a Form of Story many people hunger for; just look at the tabloids, who like nothing more than a fall from grace by a once-exalted person. Tabloid newspapers have a very good sense of what sells papers! Tabloid journalists are very accomplished storytellers - they simply use the 'facts' of other people's lives to tell their stories. Given all this, ought we not be saying, how can we best use story to introduce children lovingly to this greatest of realities?

So, how do you make a Tragedy? After all that talk from me, are you ready to make another Memory Palace? This Memory Palace requires ten locations. If you don't have a ten-room building in mind (I don't!), use different walls within rooms or objects inside your locations on which you can place Memory images. But first, you should clear out all that confetti and sweep up the balloons and custard pie mess left over from Comedy. Done? Wonderful.

By the way, you will see that one stage of this Form of Story, the second, is written in brackets. This is very important, and it's because this stage *is not to be disclosed to your listeners!* You need it for your composition, and you need to keep it to yourself because you need to leave, to your listeners, the pleasure of working this bit out for themselves. So, to begin:

1. Who, Where, and of What Qualities? - say who your story is about, where they are, and say some things about them that will make us feel they are of value.
2. (Flaw or weakness - choose for you character a hidden, fatal flaw. Keep this to yourself so the Action of the story can expose this flaw.)
3. Challenge - your character is faced with a difficult Challenge to which they alone must respond. It must be in the nature of this Challenge

that it runs directly into the nature of the character's Tragic flaw, confronting it.

4. Choice is urged - something or someone urges your character to take action in response to the Challenge. Who or what is it that so urges? Is it bad advice the character will take, or good advice the character will not take?
5. Wrong choice - and wrong action taken, because of the Tragic flaw.
6. Consequences of choice - as a result of action taken, the character's difficulties worsen.
7. Repeat the processes in stages 5 and 6, and bad consequences intensify.
8. Do it again. (This is an option, not a necessity. You can still have a decent Tragedy with only one iteration, as you will read in 'Phaeton's Ride' shortly. However, if you do iterate, you can really tighten the screw on your listener.)
9. Final confrontation - will your character face up to the Tragic flaw in themselves, thereby overcoming it and, at the same time, their Challenge?
10. Disaster - no, they nearly do, but ultimately they don't. Disaster ensues, engulfing not only the character but also those around them. Disaster causes a clean out, a purging, whereby order and balance are restored.

Example Story – 'Phaeton's Ride'

Centuries back, there lived a young man called Phaeton. You would spot him in a crowd. In the community where he lived, he stood out. Some people say he lived in Greece, others that he grew up in the mountains of Ethiopia. Either way, the people who lived around Phaeton were brown skinned, with warm, dark eyes and black, black hair. Not Phaeton. Phaeton had an olive complexion. His hair, which curled softly, was pale gold in colour and his eyes were the purest blue.

Phaeton not only stood out, he stood above. At only the age of 14 years he towered over his contemporaries and was, in fact, taller than the tallest men in the valley where he lived. And his frame, though elegant and balanced in every way, was strong and muscular for a man, let alone a youth of just 14. His face shone. But these are not the only reasons he stood out.

His mother was Clymene, a dignified woman who had come to these valleys from the coast. She was beautiful too, but not golden, like her son. Some said nice things about her and some said ugly things. Clymene had arrived in those hills carrying a heavy burden - she was pregnant. Phaeton stood out from his friends, his community, because he could not point at a man and say, 'There is my father'. Yet his beauty was such that some said he must be the son of a god! They looked at the golden sun that rose and rode each day across the sky, and looked at golden Phaeton in the radiance of his beauty, and they wondered.

When he was about 5 years old he had asked his mother, 'Mother, who is my father?'

Clymene had stopped her work (she was preparing a meal for them both), took a deep breath and said to her son, 'You are old enough to know the truth – your father is the god, Apollo.'

Phaeton was stunned! 'Apollo?' he breathed.

'Yes,' said Clymene, 'that is the truth. But you must be careful who you trust that truth to. There may come a time when your father wishes to be closer to you but for now you must tell no one that, when you see the golden sun crossing the sky, that is your father riding in his chariot, pulled by his fiery horses, and pulling the sun itself across our sky.'

Now, of course, as soon as you know a thing like that you are bursting to tell somebody, and this truth burned in Phaeton's body like the sun burnt in the sky. Sometimes, the heat of it was so much that he felt he would be quite unable to keep it in, that he must open his mouth and let something of its radiance escape, for fear of burning from the inside. Sometimes, he longed to just open his mouth and vomit out its dazzling glory, blinding himself and all around. But his mother told him that, if the god himself did not publicly acknowledge his son, then the god's counsel must be kept.

'It is your secret, my love,' she said, 'but it is not yours to tell. That is for your father, *if* and when he chooses.'

So Phaeton kept the secret, but every night, tucked up in his little bed, he would imagine those great horses, now stabled for the night, that huge chariot waiting silently and then he would imagine the harnessing, the yoking, the coupling of that chariot to that great burning disc of the sun and the god, his father, stepping into the chariot, planting his feet on the boards of it, gathering the reins, raising up that flickering whip, lashing the horses into a gallop, and the miracle of sunrise! Sometimes, he imagined himself inside that chariot beside his father. No, not sometimes; nearly always he imagined that.

Years passed and Phaeton grew, taller than his contemporaries, stronger than his contemporaries, brighter than his contemporaries, so much brighter that even mature women shaded their eyes when they saw his beauty. Still that secret burned inside him, but he let no flare of it escape.

Then, when he was not quite 15, he was down at the river with his friend Epaphus. Epaphus had recently turned 16, though, in growth, he looked like a child next to Phaeton. He had celebrated his birthday and was boasting to Phaeton of all the gifts his family had given him.

'Look,' he said, 'my uncle gave me this fishing rod, and today we are going to catch fish with it! And look, see what my father gave me!'

He showed Phaeton a strong knife.

'When we have caught a fish, my knife will open it up as if it were slicing butter. See, it's really sharp, a man's knife!'

He tested the edge, the point, with his fingertip, then gave it to Phaeton to admire, 'It's made of bronze,' he said. 'See, it shines like the sun shines!'

Phaeton inspected and admired the knife.

'My father,' Epaphus continued, 'says that next year, when I'm 16, I will be a man and he will give me my first shave!'

Phaeton nodded.

'But you won't be 16 for ages! You're not even 15 yet!' Epaphus went on, 'and you won't get given a knife until ... oh, well, you won't, will you? Because you don't have a father!'

Phaeton was unable to breathe, and he felt the blood heating his face.

'You can't get a knife, because you've got no father to give it you!' gloated Epaphus, and something hidden deep inside Phaeton burned as if it had been stoked.

'Ha! Ha! Ha!' Epaphus laughed, 'maybe your mother will give you some knitting needles! Some woman's thing for little Lack-Daddy!'

'I do have a father!' snapped Phaeton.

'Well of course you do, somewhere!' taunted Epaphus. 'Somewhere in a fishing port, probably drunk and stinking of fish! But you don't know who he is and I dare say your mother doesn't know either!'

'My father is the god, Apollo!' said Phaeton. That was it. All those years of keeping it in and in the end it was so simply said. It was said now, couldn't be unsaid. But this didn't improve matters.

'*Apollo!*' screeched Epaphus, beside himself. 'Is that what your mummy told you!? Or is that what someone told her? "Don't worry, pretty one, it's alright, I can take care of things because, after all, I'm the god Apollo! I may look like a fisherman, but this aroma of raki and fish guts is merely my *disguise*! I'd get in no end of trouble if I went around the stews of this town in my immortal form, so I have merely adopted this disguise to spare me the aggravation! So, you can, you know ..." Ha! Ha! Ha!'

Phaeton grabbed his friend by the front of his tunic, drew back his fist. Epaphus raised his hands, palms out in a gesture of warding, 'If Apollo is your dad, prove it!'

Phaeton remembered his mother's words – this secret was not his, but the god's, to broach. Too late. He could, he thought, just smile, release Epaphus, and say that Epaphus was right and he didn't know who his father was. It was only, he knew, what everyone around had long assumed to be the case. He knew, deep inside himself, that his mother wouldn't lie to him, that she was a good woman. He knew that people said, looking at him, that he was not of ordinary descent, that he must be the son of a great man, a prince or a king. Just look at his strength, his beauty! And he knew that some of the women said he looked like a demigod! Some of them had even said so to him, older women, who seemed freer to speak their minds than younger women, 'Phaeton, you look like you are of the race of Olympus! You are a very lucky boy, gifted with such beauty! Truly, you're divine!' But they'd meant that as a compliment rather than as the simple truth. So he could laugh, brush it off. Epaphus was often teasing people and then, seconds after it nearly became a fight, was back to being his silly, gobby friend and no harm done. This would be so easy to brush off.

'I will prove it,' he said, then turned his back on Epaphus and walked away.

He walked away and began the long walk up the great hill that rose, rocky and rubble-strewn, behind his village. He walked and walked, asking himself how he could prove to Epaphus that he was truly the son of Apollo. Not just Epaphus - everyone. He reached the summit of that hill. Below him were the creases and crevices of the deep valleys, wooded, populated. Here he was above the trees, above the people, above the world. He breathed deeply, looked up into the bright and airy sky, and saw his father. He saw the sun in its crossing of the great sky. He imagined his father lashing those horses with his lash of flame, he saw those great horses stamping, galloping. He knew what he would do. So he walked and he walked with the sun in front of him now, he walked and he walked, always westwards.

He saw the fact that he got there at all, the fact that he found the place, as proof enough to himself. There he saw the great sun, deep red now, sinking, setting and, before it, a great golden palace. All of it was gold! Golden walls rose to a gold roof, gold roof rose to golden eaves! Great gold doors glittered and glowed and all was glory, glory, glory! Phaeton was elated. He heard the roaring of the sun, like a mighty forge furnace, he heard great echoing hoof-steps, he heard the creaking of immense doors, four great whinnying horse voices, the creaking of those doors again, and then total darkness fell. He had come to his father's palace.

His eyes grew used to the sudden darkness. He began to pick out the looming hulk of the palace and then, as he edged, with difficulty, towards it (because his feet missed the darkened path) the moon rose, a bent silver bow. He stopped and gazed; the moon, Artemis, his father's sister, was helping him. His auntie! He giggled.

Reaching those high doors, he knocked, startled by the great echoing boom his knocking made. He waited. The huge door creaked slowly open. There stood a beautiful woman, tall, slim, gossamer-clad. She smiled and, without a question, welcomed him in. She'd smiled like she knew him. He followed her down vaulted corridors that were lit with torches and then towards a great hall that glowed as if with a thousand torches. But there were no torches in that hall, only Apollo.

Apollo sat in his golden throne, mopping his brow, refreshing himself with a cool drink. He looked up, saw Phaeton and knew him.

'Ah!' he said, and his voice made the hall throb with its resonance, 'you have come to me, my son!'

Phaeton could have wept then, but he didn't.

'I am truly your son, then?' he said.

'You are,' said Apollo, 'haven't you always known it?'

'Yes!' gushed Phaeton.

'Don't you know it in the deepest part of you, deep in that part that no man can touch, nor plunder? Where no man can take that knowledge from you, because it is who you are! Don't you know it there?'

'Yes, father,' said Phaeton, 'and yet ...'

'I am glad to see you! Of course, I have seen you every day of your life, as you have seen me, and I am proud of my son. And now you have come to me and I am overjoyed! Let me give you a gift! Name anything you want from me, and, by All-Father Zeus, I will give it to you!'

Phaeton paused, fidgeted a little, and then, 'Father, tomorrow, let me ride your chariot! Let me drive your team and let me draw the great sun through the sky!'

Apollo was shocked.

'No,' he said, 'choose again! Anything but that!'

'I have chosen, Father, and you have sworn, by Almighty Zeus.'

'Yes, but Phaeton, no man, still less a youth, can possibly drive my chariot! There is not even any god but I can hope to master my team of horses, not even Zeus! I beg you, choose anything but that.'

'I choose that.'

'I can make you a king! I can make you a great ruler, commander of ten thousand men. Your ships will blot out the horizon, the spears of your hoplites will out-bristle the greatest forest! I can give you that and more.'

'I have spoken my wish, and you have sworn,' said Phaeton. He could hear Epaphos' laughter.

Apollo climbed down from his throne, took his son's shoulders in his hands. 'Will you make a god beg, Phaeton? To drive my chariot will mean your death.'

'It will not!' said Phaeton. 'You said no man can drive your chariot? I am not a man! You've told me, I am your son, I am half-divine. Your nymph at the door knew me, you knew me, your horses will know me too.'

Apollo saw that Phaeton would not change his mind and knew that, yes, he had sworn by Almighty Zeus. No man can go against his oath, and nor may a god. He spoke now to his son in a low, an urgent voice, 'Tomorrow then, you will make the sun rise. But Phaeton, don't drive too close to the Earth or you will burn her. And don't drive too high either, or Earth will freeze. Master the horses, hold them in your command, or all living things will suffer.'

'Yes, Father,' said Phaeton.

Hours later, the world still quilted in darkness, Phaeton walked towards the stables where he would meet his father. As he walked he heard light, quick footsteps and, turning, saw the beautiful nymph who had opened the door to him. She rushed up to him.

'Phaeton,' she said, 'please don't do this! You will come to harm and I couldn't bear that!'

He frowned, mumbled something, resumed walking. She hurried alongside him, saying, 'I beg you, Phaeton, please? I've known of you all your life, I've watched over you all your life and all your life I've longed for the day when you became a man. For personal reasons I've longed for that Phaeton! You have only to wait a few more little years and you will be a man, and we ...'

'Manhood,' snapped Phaeton, 'is not a thing you wait for, it is a thing you seize. I'm seizing it now as I will shortly seize the reins of my father's chariot.'

He moved on and she came with him, still urging him to stop. As they got closer to the stables the air grew hotter and hotter. She, evidently, was struggling with the heat, and, yes, it was getting very hot but Phaeton could bear it. She, apparently, could not.

'Phaeton, for my sake!' she implored, 'I can come no further, the heat ...'

'Fine, I can!' said Phaeton, and he walked on.

He reached the stable yard, and there was his father. They entered the stable and Phaeton saw the horses. They were gigantic! Their proud heads tossed. Their hoof-stamp was deafening. Their pale coats gleamed, their necks arched with strength, their golden manes rippled iridescently. They were already harnessed and yoked. Apollo himself took the great long traces from the back of the chariot and, walking with them into another chamber of the stables, coupled the chariot to the sun. Then he gestured to the chariot, and Phaeton boarded. Apollo, looking grim, handed him his great whip. Phaeton flicked it and flickering flames flashed and flared along its length. He took up the reins with his other hand. He whisked that whip backwards and forwards, then swirled it up over his head and *whack!* With an ear-splitting, flame-shedding crack, he was off! The horses hauled at that great chariot, hauled at their great load, and stepped from walk into trot into canter and then all out and into glorious gallop! Phaeton spread his feet as wide as he could to brace himself against that speed as the chariot streaked out of its stables. And far above the Earth, the Sun rose.

The thunder of the horses in front, the great burning roar of the sun behind and the hot wind in his face exhilarated Phaeton. He whooped, he hollered, he yelled and he hooted for the sheer, wild joy of it! He whipped and he whipped, glorying in the power he held, and drove those horses faster and faster. On Earth, people saw the sun rising like a charging lion, all power, all speed, all fire and glory! Phaeton was dizzy with joy. The horses were strong, but he held them. The speed was immense but he stood firm against it. The heat was savage but Phaeton endured it. Far below, he saw the world. Below and in front he saw the black ocean glowing first with red, then shimmering with gold as *he* approached it. Far off he saw the snow-capped mountain tops catch fire with the sun's glory, he saw the wide plains bask in *his* light. Then, he recognised his own home country. He saw that tall hill behind his village, but now it seemed no bigger than a pimple. And he thought, 'If I stay at this height, Epaphus won't be able to see it's me driving my father's team. He won't see that I have made the sun rise ...'

So he directed the horses to run lower, to dive over his home valley. Just think, he thought, when people saw him!

What people saw was the sun growing bigger and bigger. What people heard was the roaring of a thousand furnaces. What people felt was an unbearable heat growing hotter and hotter. In agony, they tore off garments, now unbearably hot, and their skin blistered and burned. Their animals stampeded in panic. People ran for shelter in their houses, hoping for shade under their roofs and then their roofs burst into flames. Crops crackled and burnt. Trees burnt like great candles, meadows were incinerated and rivers and lakes boiled away, hissing, into nothingness. Seeing this, Phaeton hauled on the reins, dragging the horses' heads upwards and now they climbed and climbed. Higher and higher they climbed and beneath him, behind him, streams froze. Snow fell on summer flowers, snow buried paddocks, houses, entire villages, and still Phaeton climbed. From the mountains, huge glaciers now gripped the ground, grinding, grating. Villages that shivered in the paths of these glaciers were buried, crushed by their weight.

When, at last, Phaeton saw this destruction, he directed the horses again to dive, but now they broke out, rebelled, and he could no longer hold them. Now the sun was seen to careen and crash around the sky. The peoples of the Earth screamed and screamed. Apollo, watching, saw this, heard this, and wept for his son, wept for the Earth and damned himself for his mistake. Almighty Zeus saw this too, and frowned.

Standing with each of his feet on two mountain tops, mighty Zeus stared frowningly at the rampaging sun. He raised, in his massive hand, his crackling thunderbolt. Apollo saw him, saw what he meant to do and gasped out, 'Father, I beg ...'

But what could he say? He watched, agonised, as Zeus stretched back his great arm and *crack!* He flung his lightning bolt into the air. It flew straight at the sun, and with a boom of thunder that rolled around the whole world, it hit its target. Phaeton was obliterated. The horses, no longer whipped to madness, found a gentler pace and trundled their way back home to their stables. The world breathed its relief.

Apollo would never again let anyone drive his chariot, and never again would he swear a hasty oath. Epaphus would never tease anybody again, ever. And Clymene?

Clymene never again smiled at the rising sun.

Example Story from the Globe Theatre Telling Tales Workshop

Before the workshop I mentioned earlier in which a disparate group of children aged 5 to 11 were able to create a Comedy founded structurally on Shakespeare's Comedies, I had already been booked by the Globe Theatre to run a workshop based on the Tragedies. Structurally, this was simpler. Using the structure we have just explored, children created the following story, which I wrote down afterwards. This is very much 'bones only' - time did not allow us opportunity for further development.

Lord Dragon lived in a castle on an island. He was so big that some said he was a giant. He was so strong that some said he was a hero. He was so beautiful that some said he was like a god.

One day, a mysterious robed and hooded person came to Lord Dragon and told him that someone, somewhere, was boasting that they were stronger than Lord Dragon. Lord Dragon was amused. They said that this person bragged they could take Lord Dragon easy, any day. Lord Dragon was not amused. He demanded to know who? King Henry VIII, he was told. Now King Henry, in his youth, was strong and you don't just challenge a king to single combat, but Lord Dragon did. King Henry would be a tough opponent, the robed figure told Lord Dragon, but Lord Dragon could not lose if he fought using this spear. Lord Dragon took the spear, issued the challenge, crossed the sea to England. He noticed, when he took the spear, that the robed figure was missing a thumb.

For days Lord Dragon practised with the spear. On the morning of the fight he wasn't feeling himself. Actually, he was feeling ill. He was approached by a white-haired old lady. She told him that the spear had been poisoned, its shaft soaked in the spit of leeches and the blood of anacondas. The woman could see the veins of his arm had turned a funny colour and if the poison reached his heart he would die. She could give him the antidote. But Lord Dragon ignored the advice and soon the fight was on.

Lord Dragon and King Henry were well matched and they fought hard but eventually Lord Dragon had King Henry at his mercy. But something distracted him. Looking up he saw the white-haired woman again. He saw she was missing a thumb. He saw her rubbing her head in anxiety as she watched the fight, hovering with a bottle of antidote. He saw her hair slip back – it was a wig! Beneath the wig was dark hair and Lord Dragon saw she was missing an ear! Lord Dragon realised that he recognised her, that she was in fact his estranged brother with whom he had quarrelled years ago!

The distraction proved fatal. King Henry threw Lord Dragon and wrested the spear from him, then drove its point into Lord Dragon's chest. Dying, Lord Dragon asked, 'Why did you do this?' His brother answered that his plan was to create a situation in which he could save Lord Dragon's life and earn his forgiveness. 'But you have been my death!' said Lord Dragon. 'And mine!' said King Henry, realising the poison was in his blood now. With that, King Henry struck the brother with the spear and so they all died.

A magical Tragedy of plot twists and disguises that, in the finest of Shakespearian tradition, left all the protagonists dead and the children who'd created and killed them beaming with happiness! All of the ideas for content came from participating children – all I did was keep them to the structure, and this took a little less than an hour to create and relate together. Not bad, huh?

Example Story from the Shakespeare Festival, Germany

In May 2024 I made a third appearance at the International Shakespeare Festival in Neuss, Germany. I walked on stage to a capacity house in the Globe Theatre, Neuss, with very little idea of what I was going to say. It was another live storymaking event but this time with an adult audience. So, I told them that I had the narrative structure of Shakespeare's Tragedies lodged in my brain and that we would work together; me, them, Shakespeare, to collaboratively create a new story.

I asked who our story was to be about? A man? A woman? A ... and my banter was interrupted by a very assertive voice that said 'trans person'.

'Great,' I said. 'Now, what about them? Who are they?'

In a very few minutes the audience agreed that our story was to be about a young (early 20s) transgender person who was the orphan of a diamond dealer family in fifteenth-century Venice. I briefly described Theodore's childhood – an uneasy relationship with their father, a loving one with their mother.

When Theodore was very little and their mother was washing them and, looking carefully at her child's body, she said, 'You are well named Theodore. Your name means "beloved of God" and, as I look at you, I see this is true! Because you are like one of God's angels, neither male nor female...' (in the questioning and devising stage, when the audience gave me the name 'Theodore' I silently thanked my luck!)

The family were all dead and their business was ruined, so this orphan, who had known wealth, was now extremely poor.

Theodore was desperate to be a successful actor. They had a very good singing voice, beautiful green eyes, but they were terrible at dancing. They were good natured, too much so, with a tendency to accede to the wishes of others.

The audience decided, in response to my brief and simple prompts, that Theodore was approached by an older man, a theatrical promoter. Theodore had been struggling with their training (the dancing) but this man said their dancing was original and their voice and eyes were exceptional. He would like to cast them in a new production he was developing. Theodore was overjoyed. The promoter suggested that, as they needed funding, Theodore might want to write to the families who used to be friends and associates to their ruined and now dead family. Nobody had done anything to help the family in their financial difficulties. In fact, they had been cast off by their friends as they became poor and when, due to distress and terrible living conditions, the family succumbed to sickness, none of their former friends and associates had done anything to help them. Theodore was reluctant, but the promoter kept returning to it until Theodore finally wrote a round robin letter.

It worked! These rich families were only too happy to put money into this production. Wishing Theodore much luck, they made generous donations and the scale and ambition of the production ballooned. Excitement began to build in the press and, of course, for Theodore. At this point the promoter seduced Theodore and they began a relationship. The producer cast Theodore as lead in this new production and urged them to write more fund-raising letters.

As rehearsals intensified and the dance part was still proving a challenge, Theodore was one day shocked to see the promoter with another young actor, rehearsing them in Theodore's part. Theodore blazed at the promoter, accusing them of treachery. No, the producer said, this show is going to run and run and you will need an understudy. In fact, the producer said, you can help train them. Theodore agreed and the understudy learned well. Learned the dance steps very well. Good, said the producer, don't forget to send more fund-raising letters.

The producer also told Theodore about an opportunity to do some outreach work. In the Convent of Santa Maria the nuns were caring for children, orphans, and wouldn't it be wonderful for these orphans if they could meet someone who, like themselves, had lost their family, and who was now about to become the most famous actor in Venice? Theodore agreed and went to the convent to work with the children. It was only after they got there that they learned all the children had cholera. Theodore was scared. If they got sick it was only a couple of weeks to their opening night! But when the nuns told Theodore what a difference it would make to the children, Theodore went along with it.

And got sick. Dangerously, life-threateningly sick. They struggled and struggled to get well as opening night approached but, when cholera has you it has you and so, when opening night came, the understudy took to the stage as Theodore lay sweating and delirious in bed.

The understudy was a smash hit, took the part, the praise, the fame, took everything that Theodore had dreamed of. The promoter did not visit Theodore. The promoter stopped paying rent for Theodore's apartment and, as they convalesced, Theodore, jobless, friendless, homeless, found themself in the company of other trans people in sixteenth-century Venice. They lived communally and made money by sleeping with men, who used and misused them, abusing them, beating them. The members of this community condoled with Theodore and told them they should take back what was taken from them.

A year later, the promoter was at the theatre with his star actor. An orange seller was making their way around the boxes selling candied fruit and fresh oranges. When they got to the promoter's box they locked eyes with the promoter. It took the promoter a moment to recognise Theodore, those green eyes. When he did, he was terrified. Theodore drew a knife. The promoter hid behind the star actor and Theodore, in stabbing the promoter, also stabbed the star actor, who also drew a knife. The performance had to stop because of the screams and shrieks coming from that box and, when theatre stewards rushed in they found the promoter dead, the star actor dead and Theodore bleeding out.

All of the above was generated and performed in less than an hour (I had done some character-based improv to warm us up) and I still had time for another back story[26] to finish up. All the content ideas came from the audience as I asked them prompt questions using the Tragic structure shared in this book, so that would be © Giles Abbott, © the audience, Neuss, Germany, and © William Shakespeare, all rights reserved 2024. Five curtain calls later and they let me go.

You can easily use these techniques yourself to collectively create with children or adults new and gripping stories that have never been told before. You might be a teacher with children on a bus, a family, or a group of actors or creatives with the need to devise material. This work works.

7

Discovering the Monster

Like Tragedy, the Discovering the Monster Form of Story is very much around us today. It's a popular genre for films as well as books and it also shapes stories in the media (the tabloid press in particular are very skilful at selecting from the events of people's lives in such ways that the Forms of Story are highlighted). Discovering the Monster often shapes the horribly compelling content of news stories, particularly around the abuse of the vulnerable, be they women or children (stranger danger in general, Operation Yewtree in particular). The key to this structure is that, at the start, everything appears to be fine.

However, Discovering the Monster can be treated in different ways. You can either tell a story that can really unsettle, frighten and thrill, or you can make it funny. A Monster can be horrific or hilarious depending on how you treat it. So, *The Silence of the Lambs* or *Dracula* (the novel) would be examples of the former just as, at the right age, is 'Little Red Riding Hood'. But what about a simple childhood game like Grandmother's Footsteps? In the more innocent versions, the Monster, when discovered, is fled from with lots of happy squeals and is safely escaped from or, if it catches you, no real harm is done. In the more mature versions, the squeals are far from happy, consequences are grave and the Monster has to be destroyed. But the pattern that builds up to the encounter with the Monster is essentially the same.

Of crucial importance is that, to begin with, everything is fine. Then disquieting signs begin to appear that something somewhere is not fine. Did Grandmother just have a funny look in her eye? Did she have quite such hairy ears last time we visited? The protagonist initially ignores their doubts, but ultimately, has to acknowledge the very real presence of a very real Monster. Many modern thrillers are based on this structure (*Die Hard* Nos 1–94 inclusive), and so too are many murder mysteries. Murder mysteries do interesting things, not so much with the Form of Story as with the type of plot, but we'll come to that later, when we've covered all the Forms Of Story.

So, who is Monster? Well, Monster is everything you don't want to meet, don't want your children to meet. Monster is the summation of all those qualities diametrically *opposite* to the qualities you would hope to instil in a child. Monster is selfish, is greedy, is violent, is cruel. Monster can be cunning but is ultimately outwittable. There are numerous troll stories from Norway, for example, in which huge, monstrous trolls are outsmarted by plucky children. Even when Monster is fiendishly intelligent, Monster usually overlooks one crucial weakness, because of their arrogance, their vanity, or some other such monstrous quality. You won't escape me now, Mr Bond. Oh bother, I overlooked the way that you would be able to use the razor-sharp edge of the blade, descending from above you in pendulum-like swings, to first sever your own bonds and then those of my gasping secretary, and then escape, by a hair's breadth and then, by means of her hairpin, turn my nuclear-powered plasmic oscillator into a ... and in my monstrous conceit I've just told you my entire plan! You kind of know this one already, don't you? And yet we all turn up in our millions to watch it again! Our lifelong relationship with this Form of Story starts in childhood and stays with us through our whole life's journey as we begin to pass beyond the phase where everything is fine and begin to notice, subtly at first, that everything is not fine; in fact, there are undeniable signs that things are far from fine.

So, where do you start when creating your own Discovering the Monster story? By creating another Memory Palace? Ah, not so fast, Mr Bond, I have another little treat in store for you ...

Monstrous Logic

You will, of course, already be aware (you learned this in Tragedy) that sometimes, when you create a story, there are certain things that you must, at first, keep hidden. The key thing in Discovering the Monster is that the Monster must become apparent gradually, giving the listener the pleasure of feeling that something is wrong before they are told so. It doesn't hurt a story if it can flatter its audience - quite the opposite. So, the presence of Monster is first suspected by its effects, but doubted, then doubted again, until something makes it horribly clear that something in the world is wrong. This is why I call this form *Discovering* the Monster and not Overcoming the Monster, which could simply be a Quest. In fact, just as we earlier learned that just because a story is funny does not mean that it's a Comedy, and that just because a story is sad does not mean that it's a Tragedy, it is important to point out that just because a story has a Monster in it does *not* mean it is a Discovering the Monster story. The story of 'Perseus and Andromeda', for example,[27] for all that it features a Monster, is not a Discovering the Monster story. There is nothing hidden, nor insidious about the Sea Monster in the Perseus story; it is as regular and expected as the arrival of swallows in summer and the chaining of women to the rocks is an annual event like the Chelsea Flower Show. The key to successfully creating a Discovering the Monster story is to first create your Monster, then hide it, and then tell the story of your characters' journey from blissful ignorance, to doubt, to suspicion, to conviction and lastly to confrontation. It's much more fun for your listeners this way because they go on the same journey, and before they actually meet the Monster they have the deep experience of anticipating it, of imagining what or who it might be. Dread and foreboding - pure storytelling gold!

You will, of course, also be aware that the most failsafe way to create a Monster is through the application of monstrous logic and that this particular branch of logic was invented by Aristotle in Ancient Greece in the fourth century BC. Alright, I admit that this is probably not what Aristotle had in mind as its primary application when he created what is known as Aristotle's *10 Categories of Being*,[28] but it really works and it makes full, vivid, grotesque and horrible Monster creation really successful and really fun! Let's start.

At some point, twenty-four centuries ago, Aristotle turned his meticulous mind to a particular question - in how many ways is it possible to know any particular thing? He concluded that there are ten ways, namely:

1. Its Substance - what is it in its essence?
2. Its Qualities - what about it? The things you can say about it that cannot be removed from it; so, its colour, its texture.
3. Its Quantity - what about it can be described numerically? Height? Weight? Length? Number? Age?
4. Its Relation - what other things is it connected to or part of the family of?
5. Its Location - where is it?
6. When is it?
7. What is its Posture? Is it standing? Sitting? Lying?
8. What does it Have or Wear? These are not Qualities (like antlers or eye colour) that are permanent, inextricable, because Qualities of Having/Wearing must be things that can be removed from it, so for example, a hat, a beard, a snood (well, you never know....), a belief or opinion.
9. What is its Action - what does it do or is it doing?
10. What is its Passion - the opposite of Action, not what it does but what is done to it?

So, now, let's use these categories to create a Monster. Please read just one, respond to the question with your full imagination, and only then move on to the next.

1. Substance. What is your Monster? E.g., a vampire? An animal (real or made up)? A murderer? An exploiter?
2. In Quantity, what can you measure about your Monster? How many arms/eyes, for example? What age? Weight?
3. What are some of its Qualities? Is it, for example, Strong? Sneaky? Greedy?
4. Relation - does it belong to a wider group of monsters, e.g. Trolls, Giants? Does it have a monstrous mother/family?
5. Location - where is it? Living up the street? Under the stairs? In that creepy castle? In the back of a battered white van?
6. When is it? Now? Years ago? In the future?
7. What is its Posture? Is it standing on one leg? Flat on its belly? Hanging upside down?
8. What does it have or wear? A visor? A sword? An axe? A hoodie? An apparently charming smile?
9. Action - what is it doing?
10. Passion - what is happening to it, which, of course, includes the question, what is it feeling?

So, what have you got? Is it horrible? That's wonderful! Now, where are you going to hide it and who is going to Discover it?

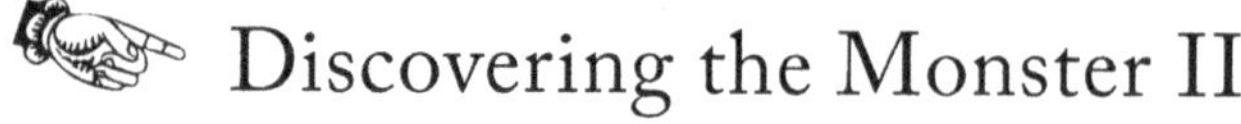

Discovering the Monster II

Now it's time to build a Memory Palace. Somewhere in this palace you are going to hide your Monster. So, remembering that the main protagonist(s) of your story is *not* the Monster but the person or people who are going to discover the Monster ...

1. Who and Where - choose who your story is about and where they are. At this stage, everything is fine!
2. Signs of Imbalance - your protagonist notices that something seems odd. What is it?
3. Doubt - your protagonist is uncertain of their perceptions.

4. Further signs of imbalance - and your protagonist is now convinced that something is wrong.
5. Disbelief - your protagonist shares their misgivings with others and is met with disbelief. No one agrees that something is wrong.
6. Loss - something or someone of great value is lost because of Monster and Monster's existence is thus proven.
7. Hunt - for the Monster. This is the beginning of a Quest that can be very brief (go straight to 8) or it can be expanded fully, which would look like:
   - 7.1. Journey
   - 7.2. Friend/Help
   - 7.3. Enemy/Obstacle
8. Confrontation - with the Monster.
9. Result - does your protagonist defeat/destroy the Monster? Or does the Monster escape, thereby queuing up a sequel?

I've run this workshop with children and we have had outlandish Monsters but perhaps my absolute favourite was a group of 11-year-old girls who created a story set in nineteenth-century London in which the Monster was cholera caused by bad plumbing. They made a genuinely moving story, displayed all their learning on Bazalgette and plumbing, and sometimes realism is a harder illusion to pull off than the fantastical. This also shows clearly how these storymaking techniques can enhance curriculum delivery in other subjects such as history, sociology, politics and more.

Example Story – 'Mr Fox'

This is a story I have told many times over the last decade to 11-year-old schoolchildren as well as to adults. Children of this age often demand a scary story, so I tell them I am going to tell them a story about something truly scary. I am going to tell them a story about love. They groan resignedly and I begin to tell them this. Shakespeare's Benedick, in Much Ado About Nothing, *quotes the refrain of this story and I like to tell children, who sometimes break into spontaneous applause at the end, that they have just been scared by a story that, some 500 years ago, will have frightened the young William Shakespeare, who has Benedick refer to it as 'that grand old tale of Mr Fox'. In other words, that grand old tale that everybody knew so well that there's no need at all for Benedick to go into detail.*

A long time ago, in England, there lived a young woman whose good luck was her misfortune and whose greatest mishap was a blessing. Her name was Lady Margaret.

Lady Margaret was the eldest of six children and she had five younger brothers. You might think that this is both blessing and trouble enough but it goes further than that. When Lady Margaret was 7 years old her mother was brought to bed with another child and, sadly, although the child, a boy, lived, Lady Margaret's mother died whilst giving birth. Now, that's a misfortune, isn't it? Then, seven years later, when Lady Margaret was 14, her father fell off his horse when hunting. He landed on his head and he died. So, to have no mother and father at only the age of 14, that's a misfortune, isn't it?

It was, and Lady Margaret felt it to be so and yet, in a strange way, it was good luck too. In the times when Lady Margaret was alive girls got married when they were young and mostly they married a man their father chose for them. Lady Margaret didn't have a father now to order her to marry anyone and so, because she didn't want to marry, she didn't have to marry. She wanted to ride horses and go hunting and fishing with her brothers. She wanted to stay out overnight on the moors with her brothers and, because she was the eldest and had almost been mother to her youngest brothers, her brothers respected her and, if she wanted to do something, as far as they were concerned, she could do it.

Lady Margaret watched as all the young women of her age were married off, some for money, some for land, some for honour. Some of them found love after they were married, but none of them married for love. Lady Margaret, aged 14, wasn't really thinking about love herself, only that, if she didn't want to think about it, then she didn't have to think about it. So she didn't.

One thing Lady Margaret did love to do was dance. In the county where she lived there were often big dances. For years, Lady Margaret loved to go to balls and to country dances. Lots of people asked her to dance. As she got older, people started asking more of her. It was really embarrassing! Men started asking for her hand in marriage.

When it first happened, Lady Margaret got all flustered and stammered and stumbled a lot and it took a long time to find the right words to carefully and politely frame the *'no!'* that had started screaming in her head as soon as she had heard the question. But honestly! Sir William was so old! But once this had started it didn't stop and soon Lady Margaret was being proposed to at every dance she went to and it began to take the fun out of going out. Men kept telling her she was beautiful and that they could make her very happy. She always wondered how they could be so certain they could make her happy if they didn't know her, and they didn't, not really. How could men always be so confident?

Years passed and Lady Margaret grew into the full bloom of her womanhood and, actually, she really was beautiful, very beautiful. She was also wealthy, intelligent, respected by her peers and respected and loved by her brothers, so she was quite a catch. Most attractive of all, she was free!

Now gentlemen were calling at the house, every month at least. They'd arrive, shake hands with her brothers, do a lot of smiling. Everyone did a lot of smiling because nobody knew what else to do. Why was Sir Henry here? Then Sir Henry, or Sir Harry, or Sir Herbert or Sir Humphrey or Whomever would mutter a few words to Lady Margaret's oldest brother, who would mutter a few words back and all the brothers would leave the room. Lady Margaret would realise, too late, what was happening but here she was again, stuck in the room with a smiling and unwelcome suitor. Sometimes she thought, 'Do these men have no idea of themselves?' as gentlemen of great antiquity would, with greater difficulty, go down on one knee, make obviously memorised speeches about their sincere affection, little speeches about how their dear departed first wife, Lady Whateverhernamewas, had died tragically young but had begged Sir Whatsisface to be happy and anyway, that was six months ago now ... By now, Lady Margaret had got very good at saying '*no!*' and these gentlemen left, muttering to themselves that she was 'too proud', leaving behind them an aroma of disappointment, indignation and parma violets.

One day, Lady Margaret's oldest brother, Richard, said to her, 'Come on Maggie! You going to have to get married one of these days, aren't you? You're 23 now! Getting to be an old maid!'

Lady Margaret was aware that most of the women she knew of her age had already been married for years and that some of them even had sons who would start shaving in a few years.

'I will get married one day,' she said, 'but I'm waiting for someone, you know, different, someone special.'

'Oh Maggie!' said Richard, 'do you think that's wise? I mean, Mum and Dad seemed very happy together and would you say that Dad was special? You and I were old enough to get to know him, weren't we, and he was very nice, very kind, but would you really say he was special? Or that Mum thought he was special?'

Lady Margaret couldn't answer. She looked out of the window at the light rain now beginning to fall on their estate. Gosh, she thought, how tall that beech tree had grown since she was a child!

Then, not long after that, she was at another big dance and she saw someone new.

He was different. Not shockingly, but he was definitely different. Lady Margaret noticed he was dressed in the style of the time but that his clothes were cut that bit sharper and there was less flounce, less fluff. His clothing was cleaner, simpler. He was stylish.

Then she noticed that this man didn't talk much. She watched him move from group to group and saw that he listened much, spoke little, but that when he did speak, everyone else would nod vigorously. So what he said was interesting. Lady Margaret found him interesting even without hearing what he said, so she waited for him to notice her. Because he would, and then he would come and ask her to dance, then they could talk as they danced and she could find out about this intriguing man. Of course, he would notice her and he would come and ask her to dance, she knew he would, because by now she'd learned that men always did. She sat back and waited.

She waited all evening, because he never did ask her to dance. He never even looked at her. Now, do you think this made her less interested or more interested? Of course, you're right, it made her much more interested. By the time the next ball came she had already learned that his name was Mr Fox. He was a newcomer to the county and he was very rich. He had taken residence in a castle in the north of the county. Everyone who'd met him spoke very highly of him. Margaret had taken extra pains getting ready for this ball and had made herself look so lovely that when she came downstairs to join her brothers in the carriage, even her brothers blinked. When she stepped into the ballroom, people gasped. And did Mr Fox gasp and come and ask her to dance? No. He did look at her, but only for a moment. His eyes, as he looked around the crowded ballroom, passed over Lady Margaret in the way the light from a lighthouse rakes over the black waters of the sea at night. That was all, but even so, because of that look, Lady Margaret couldn't sleep for nearly a week.

At last, at the third occasion, he did ask her to dance, and Lady Margaret thought, 'At last! Now I shall get to discover who this Mr Fox is!'

In those days, you see, dancing was really one of the only times young people could talk freely together without older people listening in. Mr Fox was a very good dancer. He held her confidently, he didn't kick her shins and he didn't tread on her toes. They turned and turned and people commented on how good they looked. But throughout the dance, Mr Fox didn't say a word! At the end, he simply bowed and went off. He was maddening.

But little by little, event after event, he would dance with her, he would dance with her more than once and, little by little, he began to talk. But here Lady Margaret had an entirely new experience. Mr Fox did talk, but mostly he didn't talk about himself; instead, he asked her questions. What really astounded Lady Margaret was that when she'd answered his question, he'd ask her another question prompted by her answer. He really listened! He really wanted to know about her! Lady Margaret had never come across this in a man before, and it made her more dizzy than any dancing ever could. She admitted it; she liked him.

So she told her brothers to invite him to the house to hunt on their estate or to fish in their stream, and they did, and he did, which is to say he came to their estate and hunted or fished, and then went home again, without coming into the house and without saying hello to Lady Margaret at all. This was maddening! Oh, her brothers were full of stories about what a fine chap he was, what a solid fellow, but all she got was the sight of his carriage arriving (very stylish, and simple as his clothes were stylish and simple; a black carriage with silver trim, black and silver wheels, drawn by six black stallions) and then the sight of his carriage driving away again.

But, little by little, he began to pop in to the house, and they'd see each other. Little by little he came to the house more and more, and more and more was becoming longer and longer in the time spent with her and less and less in the time spent hunting or fishing. Eventually, it got to the point that Mr Fox came to the house to hunt and fish but didn't do any hunting or any fishing. He just stayed in the house, talking with Margaret.

One night, at one of the large county balls, Margaret and her brothers arrived. They were saying hello to friends, talking with people. Mr Fox walked straight up to Margaret and said, 'Lady Margaret, may I ask you to mark your card to dance every dance with me tonight?'

'Yes,' said Margaret, surprised, 'but why?'

He answered, 'Because I couldn't bear to see you in the arms of another man tonight.'

And then he turned and walked away, leaving everyone to settle in. Margaret could hardly breathe.

At that ball she danced only with Mr Fox. The older women, the county gossips, watched and noticed and talked eagerly to each other. Yes, didn't they look good together, yes, weren't they an attractive couple, no, they didn't know of any understanding between them, but yes, couldn't they imagine one! The older men looked at him and looked at her and wished that they were young again. When the last dance was called, Margaret and Mr Fox danced so beautifully that all the other dancers stopped to watch. The band played the best they'd ever played as Margaret and Mr Fox twirled and spun across an empty dance floor. The last note played, the last move was made and all the guests burst into a round of applause. They were cheering, clapping, and then, suddenly, they all fell very quiet. Mr Fox, still holding Margaret's hand, went down on one knee. The whole ballroom held its breath to hear him. 'Lady Margaret, you know by now I'm not a man for pretty speeches. You are the finest woman I have ever seen. Will you marry me?'

'*Yes!*' said Margaret, very loudly, very quickly, almost before he'd finished his question. To be fair – she had been made to wait rather longer than she was used to.

Her brothers came over to congratulate them both, then all sorts of people were queueing up to offer their good wishes. Before the party broke up, Mr Fox said to Margaret, 'Margaret, my love, you will be the queen of my castle for as long as you live, I promise you, but will you allow me to rule you in one little thing?'

'Perhaps,' said Margaret, 'what is it?'

'I know ladies like to choose their own wedding dress but, as you know, I have strong views on style. I have in mind a dress I should like to see you in. Might you wear it for our wedding?'

'I don't know,' said Margaret, 'I should have to see the design.'

That week, he sent her the design, and she liked it. It was simple, elegant, beautiful. Now, life was suddenly so exciting! Mr Fox would visit and they would pass sweet time together and she would wave from a window when his carriage pulled away. Then, Mr Fox's tailor would visit and begin measuring up for the dress. It was thrilling as tapes and bits of cloth were held to her body, were considered, marked, adjusted. The tailor measured the length of her legs. He measured her around the waist. He measured her around the bust and across the shoulders. To her surprise, he also measured her from the ground to an inch or so above her head and to a distance either side of her shoulders. That must be for a train, she thought, but that's what was funny, because she hadn't seen a train in the design. She meant to ask Mr Fox the next time she saw him, but she forgot.

The dress grew and grew and the day drew nearer and nearer! Lady Margaret had a question that she did remember to ask. His visits were so lovely now! They could be so affectionate with each other, and it hurt, it wrenched, when he left! She asked him, one time, 'Darling, when we're married, where shall we live?'

'Oh, in my castle, my love.'

'Yes, but where is that?'

'Oh, it's in the north of the county.'

'Well, I know that, but I know the north country a little so where exactly is it?'

At which Mr Fox answered that she would have her whole life to learn about his castle! He changed the subject. Margaret returned to the question as soon as she felt she could and, again, he put her off, changed the subject. She felt he was dodging her question. Now, do you think Lady Margaret liked that?

Of course she didn't, and she decided she was going to teach him a lesson. She was going to teach him a lesson that was worth sorting out early on if they were going to have a happy marriage, and that was that she was not the kind of woman you could keep in the dark, or not answer when she asked you a question. She decided, next time he came to visit that when he left she would wave him off from the window as she always did, and then she would rush downstairs, throw on a cloak, leap on to a drab but strong horse, and she would follow him. She would make herself look like someone you wouldn't look at and she would follow him back to his castle. She would pack a bag with food and water and she would wait, hidden, watching his castle for when he left. When he left, she would go inside, take a good look round and memorise where everything was. Then, when they were married and she entered that castle as his wife, she would astonish him by knowing exactly where everything was! When he asked her how this was possible, she would tell him all and he would know how bold she was, how resourceful, how clever, and that she was not to be taken for granted nor kept in the dark, not ever! Wouldn't that be a good thing to sort out early in their marriage?

The next time he visited was such a sweet visit. It was now less than two weeks until their wedding day. When he tore himself away she ran to the window and waved goodbye to him, watching as his black carriage rumbled away, pulled by his six black horses. Then, as soon as he was a certain distance off, she ran, changed, leapt on a horse and followed. She giggled with mischievous excitement.

It was easy to follow him. A carriage and six horses kicks up quite a bit of dust. She didn't need to come too close. There was little danger he'd spot her behind him. Why? Well, in the old days, carriages didn't have rear-view mirrors, and if you're wondering why they didn't, just try reverse parking a carriage and six horses. Even when his carriage disappeared into the woods and she couldn't always see him, because the road got twisty, it was still easy to follow just from the noise of the horses' hooves and the squealing of the axles. She halted her horse when she saw his carriage pulling out of the woods because, at that moment, she also saw his castle.

It was a grim-looking place, grey stone breaking from the ground like a massive broken tooth. It made Margaret flinch, but then, she reflected, that was what castles were supposed to do, so you'd think twice about attacking them. She found a place where she could tether her horse in the woods and where she could watch that castle without herself being seen. This was not hard for her to do, and she didn't mind sleeping wrapped in her cloak. Because she had more freedom than many women of her time, she had often gone on long hunting trips with her brothers and had slept many nights on the bleak moors, and that was a lot more exposed and a lot less comfortable than sleeping sheltered by trees. A day or so after she started camping in the woods, she saw Mr Fox's carriage leaving his castle. There were big wooden boxes on the roof so it looked like he would be gone for a while. This was her chance!

She left her horse in the woods and ran across the open space of ground between the trees and the castle. She was just about to pass through the main gate when she stopped. Above the arch of the gate she saw, hammered into the grey stone, in Gothic script, large, gold letters spelling out the words, 'Be bold'.

Margaret stopped for a moment. But then she thought to herself, 'Well, I am bold!' and, as a motto, she liked it. She went inside.

She had expected the outside of the castle to be grim and plain, and then expected the inside to have hedges and flowers and statues. It had not. The inside was as plain and austere as the outside. This surprised her, and she realised she would have plenty to do once she was queen of this castle. 'This place is crying out for a woman's touch!' she thought. But then she concluded that all the luxurious things in a castle were hidden away in the inner keep where they were most safe. A castle was a strongbox, after all. So where was the entrance to the inner keep?

She looked around and around until she found a door, and here she stopped again. Above this door, in the same gold lettering, were the words, 'Be bold, but not too bold'.

Margaret stopped. She felt these words were meant less as a motto, more as a warning. Do you think she took the warning? Do you think she stopped there or do you think she went inside? What would you do if you were her?

Margaret went inside.

She had expected that inside there would be paintings, tapestries, carpets, vases of flowers and all sorts of soft and pretty things. There were none. The walls were bare and grey. The whole place felt like the hospice Margaret had visited where the sick and old people were taken to be cared for while they died. How could Mr Fox live in a place like this? How could he expect her to live in a place like this? She kept looking around and around until she came across another door. This door, at its tallest, only came up to her waist and above it were printed the same gold letters, only this time they said, 'Be bold, but not too bold, unless your heart's blood should run cold'.

This definitely felt like a warning. In fact, it felt like a threat. What would you do? Would you go through that door? What do you think Lady Margaret did? Do you think she's the kind of person who takes threats?

With a gulp, Lady Margaret pushed open that door. She had to crawl on her hands and her knees down the tunnel that opened from that door. As she crawled, the door slammed shut behind her. And that's when the smell hit her.

The smell was terrible! Really, it was the worst thing Lady Margaret had ever smelled. It was sickly, it was sweetish, but it was really sick-making and Lady Margaret had to swallow something back that rose up in her throat when she smelt that smell. She pulled her cloak over her nose and mouth and kept on crawling.

After a while she could stand up as the tunnel became a corridor. There was just enough light to see by from thin arrow slits in the wall. Margaret realised this tunnel or corridor must be creeping round one of the outside walls of the inner keep. It was a defensive structure that could be manned by archers if the outer keep was breached and that's why there were arrow slits that were letting in just enough light for her to see by. Of course, those days were long gone, it wouldn't be used like that now. The smell was getting worse and worse. Up ahead, she could see white sheets, laundry, hanging from the ceiling, but why then wasn't there a smell of soap, of cleanliness, of lavender? She came close to these white sheets. She could just make out, behind the sheets and in a corner, that there was a large basket with a lid. Maybe the smell was coming from in there? She determined to push through the sheets and investigate.

Now, you know the way that sheets, when they're wet, have a certain weight to them? That they can be quite heavy? Lady Margaret was expecting that but these sheets were incredibly heavy! She really had to heave to move them aside. She did, and as she stepped through, those sheets swung right back at her, forcing her off her balance, and something touched her face and Lady Margaret looked and she ... *screamed!*

The thing that had brushed against her face was a foot. A woman's foot. Painted toenails. Lady Margaret looked up and reeled with horror when she saw that the sheets weren't sheets at all. They were women. Young women of about her age. They had figures like Lady Margaret. They had hair like Lady Margaret and they were all wearing wedding dresses of exactly the same design as the wedding dress that was being finished right now for Lady Margaret. Lady Margaret saw the faces of these young women. Some of them had been there for a long time and their faces, their skin, had changed. That's where that awful smell was coming from. But worse than that, some of them looked like they hadn't been there very long at all. You might think these young women were asleep, except that they were hanging by their necks, and Lady Margaret could see expressions on their faces, expressions so awful that she couldn't bear to look! And she could also see what Mr Fox had done to their faces. She prayed he had done this after they had died, but feared he had not.

Lady Margaret thanked God that she had come here, that she had found this out about Mr Fox, but now she desperately needed to escape. She had to push her way, again, through those ghastly dead women, and then she began to make her way back down that corridor. Then she froze. Up ahead, and through the closed door, she could hear voices, a man's voice, a woman's voice. The woman sounded like she was begging, pleading. The door opened and Lady Margaret could clearly hear a young woman begging and pleading to be let go, and then she heard Mr Fox.

'What are you making such a fuss about? If I'd known you were going to talk as much as this I would never have married you!'

Then Margaret heard a thud and no more sound from the young woman. Horrified, she heard the sound of Mr Fox dragging somebody up the corridor. Margaret turned and fled, back up that corridor, back through that ghastly chandelier of dead women, and she hid in the corner behind that basket, shaking all over.

Mr Fox dragged another young woman into that secret room. The woman was coming round now. She had a figure like Lady Margaret. She had hair like Lady Margaret and she was wearing a dress just like all the others. Now Mr Fox was saying, 'Now, if you'll just give me that wedding ring, because I need it for Maggie next weekend ...'

Margaret gulped back a scream. Mr Fox was trying to get the ring from the poor young woman's finger. He couldn't get it quickly past her knuckle, so he stood up, pressed his booted foot on to her wrist and then pulled a large knife from his belt.

'Well,' he said, 'we've all seen how a butcher joints a chicken ...'

He pressed down. The girl screamed, and that finger went flying up in the air. It flew over the basket and landed in Lady Margaret's lap. It was so hard not to scream herself and Margaret had to bite her own cheek so hard she tasted blood. Mr Fox said, 'I shall find it later. For now, my darling, we have to fulfil our wedding vows! What are you whimpering about? Didn't I promise you that you would be queen of my castle for as long as you lived? You will. You just won't live as long as you might've thought. Death will come soon, sweetie, but oh how you will beg for it to come sooner.'

From her hiding place, Lady Margaret tried not to look, but she could not help but hear, as Mr Fox finished 'celebrating' his wedding. One more young woman was left with her feet turning in air. The rope creaked. Then Mr Fox said something about how getting married was thirsty work and he left that room, walked down that corridor. When she heard that door close, Lady Margaret dissolved into a violence of sobbing.

I don't know how long she hid there, but at some point afterwards she heard the sound of horses. She ran stealthily down that corridor and peered through one of those arrow slits. She was just in time to see Mr Fox's carriage pulling away. She lost no time, running, then crawling, down that tunnel, out of that ghastly castle and back into the woods, where she found her horse, still tethered in the trees. She leapt on it and galloped back home.

Her brothers were amazed to see her. They were relieved, because they'd been searching for her. They were angry, because she'd frightened them, disappearing like that. Where had she been? She told them. As she spoke

their eyes widened. They frowned and their mouths gaped. They were very quiet when she finished, and then the oldest of her brothers said, 'Well, thank God you wouldn't be put off Maggie, and thank God you wouldn't take no for an answer, because if you had ...'

Her brothers all agreed, nodding their heads. The oldest of her brothers continued, 'Well, it's your wedding day at the end of this week. We'll all be ready.'

At the end of the week all of county society was gathered in excitement at the manor house of Lady Margaret and her brothers, so excited, how lovely, what a wedding! Mr Fox arrived and he looked very handsome, everyone agreed! He moved among the guests, smiling, charming. Lady Margaret's brothers greeted him, then stood in a wide ring around him. Lady Margaret came down herself in her wedding dress and everyone gasped at her beauty. They applauded.

Mr Fox spoke.

'Margaret!' he said, 'You look so beautiful!'

She smiled.

'I've never seen a woman look as lovely as you, Margaret!' he said.

'Are you sure?' she asked.

'Never in my life!' he assured her.

'You've never seen a woman with hair like mine, with a figure like mine, in a dress remarkably like this one? Are you sure?'

'Never in my life Margaret! You are a vision! Come, let us go to the chapel and marry without delay!'

Mr Fox began to turn towards the door but Lady Margaret stopped him.

'Before we go, I must tell you about the dream I had last night.'

'A dream?' he said, 'I trust it was a sweet dream? Come! We should ...'

'It was not. In my dream, I went to your castle.'

'It was not so. Come now, dreams are for the night and today is for us to marry!'

'But in my dream I went to your castle and saw, above the gate, in gold, the words spelt out "Be bold".'

Mr Fox stood still, frowned. 'It is not so,' he said, 'nor was it so, and God forbid it should be so.'

'And in my dream I went through that gate and looked around the inner keep until I found another door, above which I saw, in gold, the words "Be bold, but not too bold".'

'It is not so, nor was it so, and God forbid it should be so!'

'And in my dream I passed through that door and looked around inside until I found a low door, above which I saw, in gold, the words, "Be Bold, But Not Too Bold, Unless Your Heart's Blood Should Run Cold"!'

Margaret then went on to recount, as if recounting a dream, everything she'd found in Mr Fox's castle.

'It is not so!' said Mr Fox, angrily, 'Nor was it so, and God forbid it should be so!' He had developed a twitch in his cheek and his hands had curled into tight fists. And Lady Margaret said, 'But it was so Mr Fox! And it is so! And here's the proof!'

She pulled from her clutch bag, can you guess? She pulled that finger with the ring still on it, the finger he'd cut off that poor young woman's hand, and the finger was pointing straight at him. All the people gasped. Mr Fox made a strange, gurgling snarl from deep in this throat and his hand flew to the hilt of his sword.

He began to draw his sword but Lady Margaret's brothers were faster. Their five swords glittered brightly in that morning's air, and they cut that murderer down. They cut and cut until there could be no doubt that he was dead. Lady Margaret stared at the heap of him. She was breathing hard and tears were stinging her eyes. But she was safe from him, and so was every woman he might have met. And so ended the murderous career of Mr Fox.

So too ends a story that, long ago, frightened a young William Shakespeare.

8

Transformation

Transformation is an intriguing Form of Story. Sometimes Transformation stories work as Creation stories, showing us how things have become the way we know them to be. So, the story of how the elephant got its nose,[29] how the spider[30] became, how the narcissus flower was created, are all Transformation stories. All 'coming of age' stories are Transformation stories as, in coming of age, a child transforms into an adult. Let's make your Transformation Memory Palace:

1. Status quo - create a world with everything as it should be.
2. Irritant or Imbalance - a character who is, either by their nature or their actions, to disturb the peace or upset the balance of things. Who?
3. Disturbance - of the peace/balance. Show us the effect on others of this character's being or actions, e.g. Arachne frightening people by boasting she is better at weaving even than Athena, Narcissus driving people crazy with his proud refusal to succumb to any suitor, the Elephant Child asking endless questions, the Vulture, with his beautiful white feathers on his head and neck, upsetting other creatures by declaring them ugly in comparison to him.
4. Repeat - this action of irritation/disturbing as many times as you wish.
5. Intervention - by greater force, i.e. God, or the gods, all the animals together, a crocodile.
6. Danger - of annihilation for the Irritator. Are they going to be destroyed?
7. Transformation - Irritator escapes destruction but is permanently changed into something/someone different. A new balance is therefore achieved.

Example Story – 'How the Vulture Came to be Bald'

I learned this story from a Yorkshire storyteller, Christine McMahon. It's been one of my favourites for years and I've used it to delight and perhaps even educate thousands of children by now. Once you've read this you may wish to do the same ...

It was a beautiful morning on the great wide grasslands of the American plain, a vast sea of grass stretching as far as your eye could ever see, further even. The sun shone. Herds of deer walked, peacefully grazing. Somewhere in the distance was a herd of buffalo grunting contentedly. On that morning a young deer was shyly asking her mother a question.

'Mum,' she said.

'Yes dear?' said her mother, head down, browsing.

'Mum, do you know that stag?'

'Which one?'

'The one with the really big antlers, you know, with the ...'

Mum's head came up from the grass.

'Oh, you mean the handsome one?'

'Yeh Mum, he's really good-looking ...'

'Yes, I know him. What about him?'

'Well Mum he was talking to me the other day and he said, well, Mum he said I was beautiful. Is that true Mum? Am I beautiful?'

Now if this young deer had been a human girl then she would've been about 16 years old. A sensitive age, I think you'll agree, and asking what, for a person of that age, can be a big question. The mother deer needed a moment to compose her response because, of course, she wanted to answer her daughter truthfully, but also wisely, and so as she paused they both heard a loud, '*Hah!*'

They turned and saw a bird, Vulture. Vulture was perched on a dead log and he was looking at them derisively. Now, you know who Vulture is, right? And you know that he has huge wide wings covered in brown feathers? You know that Vulture doesn't kill and eat other animals but he scavenges, he eats animals that other animals have killed. And you know that, apart from a collar of white feathers around the base of his neck, Vulture has no feathers at all on his head and neck? And you know that scientists say that's because Vulture needs to be able to stick his head and neck inside dead animals to get at the soft bits and if he had feathers on his neck and head then a) it would be hard for him to get his head out again and b) if his head and neck feathers were all claggy with blood and muck then he wouldn't be able to fly, right? Perhaps that's true – but there may be another explanation.

Vulture, when he saw that he had their attention, said, 'Well, I mean to say, do you have beautiful white feathers along the length of your head and neck?'

In those days, you see, Vulture had beautiful, gleaming white feathers all along the length of his head and neck. Not just that little collar at the base but all along his neck and on his head grew a great crest, a quiff, of gleaming white feathers that shone in the sunlight, that gleamed like mother of pearl. He was very beautiful.

'No,' said the young deer, 'I don't have any feathers at all ...'

'My point precisely!' snorted the Vulture. 'You are brown as mud all over and about as interesting to look at. You are not a thing of beauty and never shall you be so. You should rid yourself of that misconception at the earliest possible opportunity!'

And at that, he spread his broad wings and flew away. Now, how do you imagine the young deer felt after that? Bad? She felt terrible, and her mother had to spend a lot of time and effort to pick up her daughter's spirits after that.

This was not an isolated incident. Elsewhere on the prairie that very same morning, a young fox was sat on his haunches closely inspecting his tail. His mother asked him, 'What's wrong with your tail darling? You've been looking at it for ages? Have you got fleas again?'

'No, I don't think so Mum,' said the little fox who, if he'd been a human child, would have been about 5 years old.

'Then what are you staring at it for?' said his mum.

'Well,' said her cub, 'it's not very big or fluffy, is it?'

'No sweetheart, but you're not very big yet yourself, are you?'

'But Dad's got a really big fluffy tail, hasn't he Mum? And Dad's really handsome, isn't he?'

Mum pulled a little secretive smile, 'Yes, your Dad's got a big fluffy tail and yes, I think your father's good-looking – but you needn't tell him I said that ...'

'But Mum, when I grow up will I have a big fluffy tail like my dad and will I be good looking Mum?'

Now Mother Fox was just taking a moment to make her best answer to what, even from a little child, can be a big question, when they both heard, '*Hah!*'

And when they turned around, who do you think they saw inspecting his own reflection in a pool of water? It was Vulture.

'Well, I mean to say,' he said. 'Do you have beautiful gleaming white feathers all along the length of your head and your neck?'

'No,' said the little fox cub, 'I don't have any feathers at all, I'm a fox cub.'

'That's my point precisely,' spat the Vulture, 'not only are you ugly, you are also ginger, which is deplorable. You are not a thing of beauty and never shall you be so. You must rid yourself of that delusion at the earliest possible opportunity!'

And with that, the Vulture spread his big, broad wings and flew off, and how do you think that little fox child felt? He felt crushed and asked his mum, 'Is it true Mum, am I ugly?'

'No darling you're not! He's just a stupid mean bird!'

'But am I ginger?'

'Yes darling you are. I was going to wait until you was a bit older before I told you about that but, believe me, some people think that's a good thing ...'

So this is how the Vulture was and how he went from place to place spreading misery and anxiety everywhere he went.

Eventually, so many animals had stories to tell about how Vulture was behaving and how he was upsetting others that all the animals got together and decided that Vulture needed to be taught a lesson. They all agreed on that, but it was harder to agree on how the lesson should be taught. Luckily, Rabbit was there and Rabbit, as you know, is one of the cleverest of all the animals. Rabbit knew that Vulture didn't kill and eat animals but waited to scavenge on animals that were already dead, and so he suggested, 'Why doesn't someone lie down and pretend to be dead? We can all hide and when Vulture is just about to feed, the animal can jump up and give Vulture the fright of his life?'

If you think that doesn't sound like much of a punishment, just try and imagine your lunch, as you lift up your knife and your fork, jumping up, pulling a face at you, sticking its tongue out and running away. Wouldn't that give *you* a fright?

So the animals all agreed to this plan. But who should pretend to be dead? They all decided it should be Buffalo.

Do you know Buffalo? Huge animal, massive shoulders, neck, covered in fur, thick horns, low forehead, head like a rock. Now, does Buffalo look like a clever animal? Or a not-clever animal? What do you think? Buffalo is such a sweetheart he'd probably answer that question himself, 'No, I'm not clever at all, I'm really not good at thinking. In fact, people say I'm a bit stupid and they're right!'

And then he'd probably laugh, a great happy rumble from deep in his enormous chest. So it was agreed that Buffalo would lie down and pretend to be dead.

'Here alright?' he said, 'and don't worry everyone, I won't let you down! I won't even breathe when I'm pretending to be dead!'

So he lay down and all the animals went and hid in bushes, in holes, in hollows, up trees, in clefts in the ground, and they waited. High up above with his great wide wings outstretched, riding the warm updrafts of air that we call thermals, Vulture's sharp eyes scanned the ground until he saw ...

'Oh look!' he said to himself, 'a whole Buffalo! And there are no other scavengers there yet. I see no coyote, no wolverine, no wolf nor bear ...'

Well, he wouldn't, would he? Because they were all hiding and whispering excitedly to each other, 'He's coming, he's seen him, don't spoil it, keep still.' And they were trying to make sure their ears didn't show and that they wouldn't get the giggles. Vulture landed. Buffalo felt him land but couldn't quite work out where he was. Vulture had landed right behind the back of Buffalo's back foot. Vulture was thinking, 'This is good! With no other scavengers around I shan't have to fight for my dinner and I can eat all my favourite bits, the soft bits with no bones or sinew in them ...'

He was staring at the soft bit right between Buffalo's Achilles tendon and his ankle bone. Can you find yours? The animals were all waiting for Buffalo to jump up and give Vulture the fright of his life, but do you think he jumped up?

No, he didn't! He didn't want to spoil it for everyone and so he simply told himself, 'I'm dead. I'm dead. I'm dead.'

The animals watched in horror as ... back went those white feathers, out came that long neck, up was lifted that sharp and heavy black and *peck*! Vulture pecked Buffalo right on that soft bit between his ankle bone and his tendon. The pain went shooting up Buffalo's leg but he swallowed the pain, saying to himself, 'That didn't hurt! I didn't feel it. I'm dead and the dead don't feel anything ...'

Vulture smacked his beak a few times. He was thinking.

'No,' he thought, 'that wasn't quite soft enough. Where else can I start, I wonder ...'

His eyes travelled up the back of Buffalo's back leg until, 'I know! I know a really nice soft place!' and he began to walk slowly up the back of Buffalo's leg until he stopped, halfway up. Do you know that soft bit behind the back of your knee? Find it now. Can you imagine being pecked there, or, as it might feel, snipped by the end of a pair of scissors?[31] But do you think Buffalo jumped up? No! He was far too deep into his role!

So the animals watched in horror as ... back went those white feathers, out came that long neck, up was lifted that sharp and heavy beak and *peck*! He pecked Buffalo right on the soft bit behind his knee! The pain was ten times worse, it was terrible, but Buffalo swallowed the pain telling himself, 'I didn't feel that! That didn't hurt. I'm dead and the dead feel no pain. Come on Buffalo – don't ruin it for everyone!'

Vulture smacked his beak again. That was soft but he wanted something even softer. So his eyes travelled even further up the back of Buffalo's back leg, all the way up to the top where he saw ...

'Oh, yes! That's a very soft place, where there are no bones at all, and look! His tail has fallen at just the right angle so it won't get in my way ...'

He began to walk slowly up the back of Buffalo's back leg. Can you guess where he was heading? If he'd started at the ankle, then paused at the knee and now he's heading further up, can you guess where he's heading? The animals could and some of them wanted to stop things right now before it got any worse, but others prevented them. Some of them, even big animals like Bear, said they couldn't bear to watch. Because Vulture had walked all the way up to the top of the back of Buffalo's back leg and now he was looking, very closely, at Buffalo's ...

Go on - you say it!

Back went those white feathers.

Out was stretched that long neck.

Up was lifted that sharp and heavy beak and ...

Peck!

Vulture pecked Buffalo right on his bottom, and I don't mean the comfy bit that you sit on, I mean the little bit *between* the comfy bit (I know you know what I mean). The pain was extraordinary. The shock was extraordinary. But what happened next was even more extraordinary. Because, and I don't know if it was the pain, or the tension or just the keeping still for so long, but at the instant after Vulture pecked Buffalo right on the bit where his bottom opens and closes, a great big enormous *fart* came blasting out of Buffalo's body. It was so huge a fart that Buffalo's bottom opened wide, as wide as the drum of a washing machine, and it plastered Vulture's feathers right back in the wind of it, it rocked him back on his feet with the force of it, as it rushed out of Buffalo's body. And after that fart an even stranger thing happened.

Because you will know that, under Boyle's Law, pressure is inversely proportionate to volume? All that great rush of air out meant that the little air that remained inside Buffalo's body was now at much lower pressure than the air all around it so, following the blast of air out, there came a great rush of air in. Which means, effectively, suction. There was a great rush of air rushing into Buffalo's body to replace all the air that had left it and when that air rushed in it took Vulture's head in with it. And when Buffalo's bottom closed again, which it did, very firmly, it closed around Vulture's beak, head and neck. Beak, head, neck and all, Vulture was now stuck inside Buffalo's bottom.

Now obviously, I can't see your face as you read this, but you should have seen Buffalo's face! He leapt to his feet, gave a great bellow and went running away across the prairie. The animals were laughing and laughing, holding their ribs, falling down laughing, wiping tears of laughter from their eyes. At the times when they could see, they saw Buffalo charging across the prairie and, sticking out of the back of him, as if he'd sat down suddenly on a dishcloth and then stood up again, they could see Vulture, desperately trying to fly backwards, desperately trying to grab on to something, anything, with his claws. After a while of watching and laughing, somebody said, 'Should we get him out of there? I mean, can he breathe in there?'

And somebody said that if he could breathe the air probably wasn't that good and then they were all lost to laughter again until someone said, 'But seriously, we should get him out of there, for Buffalo's sake if for no other reason ...'

So under Rabbit's direction (remember I told you Rabbit was the clever one) the animals made an animal pyramid with big animals at the bottom and smaller animals going up until Rabbit was at the top at the height that was exactly Buffalo bottom height. The next time Buffalo came thundering past, Rabbit leapt, grabbed hold of Vulture's desperately kicking back legs and he pulled as hard as he could, and ...

Pop!

Out came Vulture. Rabbit and Vulture both fell to the ground. Buffalo didn't stop but just ran on and over the horizon. He had a lot of running to do. But the animals were gazing in amazement, not at Buffalo but at the air. The air was filled with hundreds and hundreds of gleaming white feathers, floating and flickering down to the ground. When Vulture eventually lifted his head, his head was as we know it now, a collar of white feathers around the base of his neck but the length of his neck and the whole of his head was pink and raw and bald, all the feathers pulled out by forced extraction from that tight embrace. It has been so ever since.

That is how, according to some, the Vulture came to be bald. And if you're not convinced that this is a true story, look at him now – does he look happy or grumpy? He looks grumpy. Why? Well, each Vulture knows that once upon a time they were beautiful and now they are not.

And they only have their ancestor to blame for it.

9

Dilemma and Jump

We come now to the exploration of two types of story that don't, in my opinion, have a particularly definable structure as such and so there will be no new Memory Palace. You can create the beginning and the middle of this kind of story using any of the structures you've already learned. The key to creating these stories is not in how they start or how they build but in how they finish. To create them you need to start at the end and think backwards. For this reason, I think they are not quite so easy to improvise as the other Forms of Story we've explored, to conjure out of thin air, to make up as you go along. These are Jump stories and Dilemma stories. There is a third Form of Story, Parable, which also requires more pre-planning than the others, but we'll come to Parable later.

You know Jump stories, I'm sure you do. You've heard them since you were a child. However they start, they end with a descent into an atmosphere of quietness and suspense that is abruptly broken by a sudden noise that causes the audience to jump, hence the name. I think of them more as techniques of performance than Forms of Story, and so rather than attempting to define a structure I will instead give you below a series of barebones narratives with, in brackets, some directions for how you may wish to perform them. This'll give you more than enough of an idea of how to make your own.

Jump Stories

Example Stories – 'Golden Arms', 'The Ghost of the Finger', 'Grandma's Liver'

So, let's start with '**Golden Arms**'. This folk story actually got made into a horror movie recently.

A young man, despite his mother's urging, refuses to marry, saying that he is waiting to meet someone special. Mother protests, 'You think I waited to meet someone special? Look at your father ...' [build as much or as little detail into this section as you wish, just so long as your listener engages with the young man].

Then one day he meets someone special, a young woman. In addition to her charm, her smile, her intelligence and kindness, he knows she's special because her arms are made of solid gold. She doesn't know why. No, they're not heavy, to her they're normal. The young couple fall in love and marry.

Not long after their marriage, a plague sweeps the country. She catches it and dies. His grief is sincere and intense. After the funeral he wonders how he is going to live without her, until it strikes him that he could live a whole lot more easily if he just had her golden arms. They're no use to her in the grave, surely? She'd have wanted him to have them, surely? She'd have said so if she'd had time, if she'd been strong enough. Surely.

[Paint a scene of him walking at night with a large bag, a lantern and a shovel. Allow your listener to realise, before you tell them, that he is heading for the graveyard. Have him begin digging up her new grave until 'thunk', his shovel hits the coffin lid. Quicken the pace until he has made enough space to kneel in the grave. Slow right down as he lifts the coffin lid.]

Her face is hidden by the shroud, thank God. He uncovers those golden arms. I have him apologise to her before, with his knee on her breastbone, he saws off first one then both of her golden arms. He is astonished by the weight of them. Placing the arms on the edge of the grave pit, he blows her a kiss, closes the coffin, climbs out, buries her again. Putting the golden arms in his bag, he goes home as fast as he can, thinking that, in time, he will go and live somewhere completely different, start a new life where no one knows him, sell the arms, be rich. She would want that for him. Reaching home, he puts the golden arms under his bed and, exhausted, gets ready to sleep.

He is just drifting off when he hears the noise [build up as you wish the sound of someone in his house, getting closer, until the bedroom door opens and there stands his wife]. She moves slowly towards him.

'My love,' he says, 'what has become of your lovely red lips?'

[Whisper her words] 'All gone and wasted away ...'

'And my love, what has become of your lovely rosy cheeks?'

[Make her voice even quieter, slower.]

'All gone and wasted away ...'

[Make him quiet and slow too.]

'And my love – what has become of your beautiful, golden arms?'

[Lean in close to your listener, pause, then, as loud as you can ...]

'YOU KNOW!'

You remember Jump stories now? You probably have some of your own that you remember from childhood? '**The Ghost of the Finger**' is almost identical to '**Golden Arms**' but I include it here because it goes beyond the jump-line to a punchline.

A young woman had left home to begin life as an undergraduate. She was living in a room at the top of a converted house with another student on the first floor and another on the ground floor. One night she was alone in the house for the first time. Instead of going home, she'd decided to tough it out and be a grown-up. She went to bed, read her book until, at a certain point, she turned the corner of the page over and the light off.

Outside there came a great clattering. She went to the window and saw the metal bin had been sent flying. She reasoned, it can't have been foxes – too heavy. There were no drunks or students in the street. She stared out to the dark, rainy street, seeing only the gravel path, the hedge, the street lamps, that clot of black shadow directly under the lamp.

[Look at your listener with a 'you what?' sort of look, then ask them, 'When have you ever seen a shadow directly underneath a light with nothing for it to be the shadow of?]

She looked at that shadow. [Slow down, drop your voice.] The shadow moved. [Speed up.] She leapt into bed, pulled up the covers. Outside she heard the [do this very slowly] crunch, crunch, crunch of somebody, or something, walking up the path. Then she heard a scratching sound as if someone was picking the lock of the front door and then a voice as dry as the wind through reeds [hiss this as quietly but as clearly enunciated as you can], 'I am the ghost of the finger ...'

[Now all you need do is repeat this as somebody or something does not go into the ground-floor room, nor the first floor room. Eventually, it is in her room. At each stage of its ascending of the stairs, pause and repeat, 'I am the ghost of the finger.' Next all you need do is describe her peeping from under the bed, seeing whatever you like so long as it has a long finger. It comes close. Go very quiet, prepare your listener for another and quieter hiss but his time go as loud as you can, '*I am the ghost of the finger!*'

Then, while your listener is halfway up the curtains or hiding behind their desks, adopt the sweetest voice you can think of and add the line 'Does anybody have an itch they can't reach?']

The sense of relief and also of bathos will be palpable. Young people do love this sort of nonsense – remember 'Scaring Them Silly, Because They Want You To' (on page 63).

Because you've got the hang of this now, I can be even briefer with my last example and you'll have seen enough to realise that the build is relevant only inasmuch as it sets up a chance for you, the storyteller, to create a ghostly, quiet atmosphere, then shatter it with a Jump ending. This last story was told to me by a 6-year-old girl.

'Grandma's Liver' starts with a funeral – a little girl has lost her grandmother, her mum's mum. A few days later Mum, who is not feeling herself, gives the little girl some money, tells her to go to the butcher's shop and buy some liver. The girl spends all the money on sweets. Walking home, she reflects that a) she's in trouble and b) her grandmother no longer needs her liver. One short act of grave robbery and corpse desecration later, the girl gives some liver to her mum, who cooks it and serves it for supper. Then the girl is in bed and hears a voice, 'I'm in the graveyard. I want my liver. Are you there?'

I need hardly go on. The voice repeats, getting closer and closer, until ...

Have fun with these but be aware that Jump is a trick you can really only pull off once per storytelling session.

Dilemma Stories

Similar to Jump stories, the key to Dilemma stories is not, as far as I can tell, in how they start or build but in how they finish. Dilemma stories are told all over the world but there is a particularly strong tradition of them in the Hausa region of northern Nigeria where, as I've been told, decisions are mostly made at a village level and where, therefore, it is important to know how to discuss and explore differing opinions amicably. Accordingly, a Dilemma story flouts Aristotle's contention that a story *must* have a beginning, a middle and an end by instead having a beginning, a middle and a question. The key to the question is that it must be genuinely unanswerable. As teller you pose the question, then encourage discussion of suggested solutions while always resisting any definitive conclusion. Structurally, that's it, but you can do some amazingly interesting things with this technique. Here follow some bones-only examples.

Example Stories – 'Hausa Plumbing' and 'The Goddess Gauri'

A village in northern Nigeria. Simple but highly effective plumbing – a pit, with wooden planks across it, low wooden walls for modesty and when a pit is full it is filled in and then marked out so that no one plants any crops until a safe period of time has passed.

Two babies are born at exactly the same time, both boys. The women in the village are rushed off their feet, and they and the new mothers are exhausted. The newborns, once fed, are put in a cot together. They instantly hate each other and start fighting.

Things don't improve with age. In school they have to be separated. As adults they insult each other's girlfriends, then wives, then children. One day, one of these sworn enemies goes to one of the toilets described above. The planks break and he finds himself in the pit up to his bottom lip in human emptyings. He calls for help. The person who rushes to the scene is his enemy, who says he will fetch a rock, throw it at the man's head and so be done with him forever. He fetches a rock [and when he's about to throw it, you stop the story and, turning to your listener(s) ask, 'If you were the man in that pit, what would you do?'] There is no answer to this - just have fun exploring possibilities.

Next is an example of a Dilemma story for older listeners that comes, I think, from India:[32]

A young couple marry, she leaving her valley and moving in with his family. They are happy. One day her brother comes to her house and she's overjoyed to see him but he brings bad news - their father is dying. She says she will come right away and her husband comes too. As they walk they are in a wooded valley. The brother says he knows that in that cave up there is a shrine to the goddess Gauri. Can they wait while he goes to offer prayers for his father? Yes, they can.

He climbs up, enters the shrine, sees the statue, the altar, feels the holiness of this place and also sees the gifts people have left on the altar. He has brought nothing. In an excess of feeling for the man who gave him life, he cuts his own head off as his offering.

In the valley below, after a while, the husband tells his wife to wait while he goes to see if everything is OK. He enters the shrine, same reaction. Seeing his brother-in-law's head and realising he has not been robbed, he follows his brother-in-law's example and cuts his own head off too.

Eventually the wife climbs the hill and finds the scene in the shrine. Distraught that she is losing her father and has lost her brother and her husband, she staggers downhill. What does she have to live for now? Finding a tree with appropriate boughs, she makes a rope of vines, wraps it round her head. About to jump, she hears the voice of the goddess, 'Daughter, do you have faith in me?'

'Yes Goddess!'

'And that I can do that which cannot be done? And undo that which shouldn't have been done?'

'Yes!'

The goddess instructs the woman to take mud from the sacred river in the apron of her skirt, smear it on the necks, place the heads on top and then she will see what her goddess can do. The young woman obeys and to her amazement, sees her brother and husband come back to life.

They continue their journey and she can't believe her good fortune. She walks behind watching her brother and husband talking, laughing together. Her eyes move from one to the other until ...

Gulp! She realises she has put her brother's head on her husband's body and her husband's head on her brother's body. [You now offer to your listener(s) the question that has dawned on her, 'If my husband's head is on my brother's body and my brother's head is on my husband's body, to whom am I married?']

If you tell this story to teenagers expect a riot.

So now you've seen a couple of examples of Dilemma stories, why don't you try thinking of your own impossible questions? When you've got your question, work backwards and make a story that leads to it. Gross, funny ones are the easiest way to start but pretty soon you may want to find some questions that really do apply to people's lives and now you can create a story to explore them.

Four Types of Plot

Now you have met and explored Nine Forms of Story. You have created Memory Palaces for each type and you have created at least one new story based on each Form of Story. You've shared them with someone. Congratulations! I wish now to introduce you to four simple ideas that will enable you to create, using the Nine Forms of Story you now know, a seemingly unending variety of stories. You need never tell a story in the same way twice. This is where you get to memorise four more ideas that will help you become skilled in a finite combinatorial system for storymaking.

A finite what? I know, it's a mouthful, but actually very simple.

A finite combinatorial system is a system whereby a limited number of ingredients can be combined and recombined infinitely. You already know at least one finite combinatorial system and in fact you are using it now to read this book, because language is a finite combinatorial system. There is a limit to the number of words you know but there is no limit to the number of new combinations you can make with the limited number of words you know. You may know another if you know music, because music is a finite combinatorial system.

So, a finite combinatorial system is something with limited ingredients that can be combined with limitless variety. You have learned the nine key Forms of Story. Now you are going to learn four more elements that you can use to make new and surprising combinations. You can keep surprising your listeners (which keeps them engaged - remember Fortunately/Unfortunately?) and you can enjoy the confidence of knowing that each new combination you make is made of elements that have already been proven to work.

If the Forms of Story define what happens in a story, the Four Types of Plot define *how* what happens happens. The good news is that you've already met two of them. You've been using one in every story you've made as you've worked through this book and there's another you've touched on as part of your journey.

The Four Types of Plot are:

1. Chronological
2. Flashback
3. Parallel
4. Nested

So, the one you have been using repeatedly is, of course, Chronological, in which you start at the beginning and then move through events in the chronological order in which they happen.

The second one is Flashback, in which you start at, or near, the end and then show, through a series of glimpses, how you got to where you are now. Most murder mystery stories have strong elements of Flashback, but also Parallel, which we're coming to. We start with the victim already dead, then, via a series of glimpses we learn how they came to be dead, how much volcanic hatred there is bubbling beneath the surface of this apparently respectable Edwardian family/village/train/cruise liner and why this Belgian has summoned us all to the library ...

In Parallel plots, two or more stories start one after the other but after the initial stage of each story is completed, we switch to a different story and complete the initial stage of that before swapping back or to another story. Some highly skilled examples of this technique can be found in the works of Richard Curtis. Think of the multiple and intersecting plot lines of multiple characters in films such as *Four Weddings and a Funeral*, *Notting Hill* and *Love Actually*. Remember the way a succession of Quests opened inside 'The Lindworm' and how they all closed at the same point? In all these examples the Parallel plots are running chronologically and in the same sequence but, in a murder mystery or any kind of investigative story, one plot runs forwards (the investigators) while another plot runs backwards (the investigated). It's very hard to improvise such, but when you get to the point that you wish to kick your storymaking up a notch, here's how.

The last of the Four Types of Plot is called Nested because in this plot type one or more stories are contained within another story. You've done this yourself already; do you remember the way you put a Quest inside Journey and Return? Inside Discovering the Monster? Some literary examples of this would be *The Rime of the Ancient Mariner*, in which we learn the story of the Wedding Guest, in whose story is contained the story of the Ancient Mariner; and in *Wuthering Heights*, in which we follow the story of Mr Lockwood, whose story then contains a story told by Nelly Dean, the housekeeper, who tells us the story of Cathy and Heathcliff. These are pretty simple examples of Nested plots because things can get a lot more complicated. Take, for example, the

Arabian Nights, also known as the *Tales of One Thousand and One Nights*. In these, the frame story concerns King Shahriyah, who discovers the wives and all the women of his brother's court only wait for their husbands to go out hunting before committing adultery with household slaves (course they do). Consequent to this discovery, he will never trust women and so he marries women and then, to prevent their adultery, after spending one night with them, has them executed. This goes on until Scheherazade, daughter of the King's vizier, says that she will marry the King and, by her intelligence and her storytelling, saves not only her own life but also the lives of countless other women.

This is the start of the first Nested story. She marries the King, saying she understands that Terms and Conditions apply, and she is happy to accept them. It will be worth it. But, she asks, may she beg a favour of the King? She explains that her sister, Dunrezade, loves her storytelling. She is very sad that Scheherazade will die after one night of marriage because then who will tell her stories? Can her sister stay with them that night so that Scheherazade can tell her stories before she dies? The King grants the favour and Scheherazade begins, once married, to narrate, and there follows a succession of Nested plots in which stories interrupt stories so that, when dawn begins to show, Scheherazade apologises to her sister, saying, 'But sister, my stories can only be told by night, and now that the sky is lightening I must stop, and you will never get to hear how etc. etc. etc ...'

Of course, the King is now hooked and he says that her execution may be put off for one day so she may finish her story. Scheherazade keeps this up for one thousand and one nights, by which time she and the King have at least one child of nearly 3 years of age, and only when the King says he couldn't bear to execute her does she close the loops of the stories she has currently opened. So closes each group of Nested stories she was telling and eventually so closes the Nested plot of Scheherazade herself and finally, so closes the frame story of the King, now cured of his wife-murdering tendencies.

This extraordinary collection actually derives from a Persian precedent, which in turn derives from India and the *Jataka Tales*, which tell of the previous incarnations of the Buddha. These interlinked stories are intended to demonstrate cause and effect and the relatedness of different incarnations. By the time the technique reaches Scheherazade, that original intent is long lost, but a new one is found as an extraordinary collection of stories combines some simple, some complex stories together in deliciously interwoven ways. Among other things, the *Nights* as a whole show how intelligence can overcome superior physical and political power.

So, how do we begin to explore different arrangements of plot? Well, the first thing you can do is play a game with me ...

Shuffling the Bones

Can we now go back to the Quest story you created right back at the beginning of your journey through this book? Check your Memory Palace – it's still there! Now think your way, quickly, through the bones, the simplest key ideas that will make the story work. As a tip, when I have to reach into my repertoire for a story that I haven't told in a while, I find it useful to watch it like a movie in my head. Words can come later.

Good. Now you need six pieces of paper. Alternatively, if you own a deck of cards (I don't!) just take any one ace and any cards numbered two to six. A dice won't work as we need each number to come up only once. Now, if you are playing this game on your own, you need to shuffle those cards/pieces of paper thoroughly or, if you are playing it with a partner, they shuffle for you. I recommend playing it with a partner first if you can, because it's more fun and secondly, because it is very hard to tell a story to yourself. Anyway, now that those cards/papers have been shuffled you need to either be presented with or you select for yourself one piece of paper/card, look at the number on it and *immediately* start telling your story from whichever stage of the story your card indicates. Once that stage is finished, your partner or you pick another card and you must move immediately from wherever you were to wherever the card commands. This might sound like it is hard to do but if you commit to it (and that's another reason why having a partner helps, as it gives that sense of 'live performance'), you will find that it is surprisingly easy. There is no script, after all, and all you need do is make a bridge between one section to the next. Storytelling is not so much in the elements themselves but in how you, in the act of telling, make meaningful connections between them.

For example, a version of 'Theseus and the Minotaur' might look like this, and I have used cards to randomly generate this sequence. I have written this section as I would talk, in one go and without any editing afterwards (Jack Kerouac eat yer heart out!). I've used numbers to indicate what the shuffled cards gave me.

3

Theseus boarded the ships with the other young men and women. Many wept, but he didn't. He felt the ship rocking, rising, beneath his feet. He looked out over the glittering sea. He looked back at the glittering city. He would be back. He didn't know how, but he would be back. The ropes were untied, cast off, the ship pushed away from the dock, its sails unfurled and, filling with wind, the sails pulled the ship out to sea.

They sailed for days and nights, passing island after island until they approached Crete. Getting closer to Crete, they noticed that the sea was getting more crowded with sails. They sailed towards the harbour but the harbour was so busy they had to wait permission to dock. 'This then,' thought Theseus, 'is what a great empire feels like!'

Once they'd docked, the tribute, including Theseus, chained at the wrist and waist, were marched towards the palace. Well, the soldiers who escorted them marched – the young men and women from Athens stumbled and shambled. Theseus was aware that other ships seemed to be disgorging similar cargo. Theseus saw the great building of Knossos, the walls, the fortifications, the towers, the great stone bull-horns at the main gate. They were driven inside. They were marched to a great open courtyard. At one side of the courtyard was a high and wide stone staircase, at the top of which was a dais, at the centre of which was a throne, with smaller seats set beside and around it. A great crowd of youths and maidens were being shuffled into this courtyard, being lined up, assembled. Was there to be some kind of inspection?

4

He saw her as soon as she entered. She wasn't the first to appear at the top of those stairs, nor the first to take a seat beside the still empty throne, but she was the first he really noticed. Slender she was, with toffee-brown skin. Firm-fleshed she was, taut of tone, gymnastic of build. She wore sparkling crystals at her throat, her brow, her breast, her wrists, even her ankles. Soft-footed she was, deer-like in movement. Her hair was black and glossy, bound back, but one heavy tress of it had escaped its bounds and fell languorously, and curled down her neck, just kissing her collar bone. Theseus longed to break his bounds and kiss her just there himself! She was held in high regard, he could see, and he heard her named – Ariadne.

1

Theseus was 16 years old. Born and raised by his mother near Eleusis, he had never known his father. When he was 15 his mother had led him from the village to a quiet place. She led him to a quiet, tree-shrouded place where a large boulder was then glowing with the gold of the dwindling sun. She turned to him and said, 'Darling, years ago, your father told me that when you grew strong I was to bring you here. I was to set you the test he devised for you and, if you could pass it, send you to him and he would welcome you, but if you failed, never to speak to you of him again.'

Theseus was eager to know more. His mother told him, 'Your father has left something for you and if you can get it you can claim your birthright.'

Theseus was stunned. He had a birthright?

'The message your father has left for you is under this boulder.'

Theseus looked at the boulder. Well! He would try!

So he did try, and try, and he tried from every angle to lift that boulder but it was impossible! All the while he was thinking, was his father a giant, a Titan, that he could so easily lift boulders and pop messages beneath them? Exhausted, he looked at his mother, saw the anxiety in her face. And something more. He saw, in her face, a struggle. He saw there was something she was fighting not to say, something she knew but which she was sworn not to tell him. Evidently, he was missing something. He looked at that boulder. What was it?

Then he saw, at the back of the boulder, a small rock sticking up above the grass, maybe a foot behind the boulder. He saw that, just under the boulder and between it and that rock, was a gap, a hole. He saw, just visible in the dense bushes behind that smaller rock, a strong stick, like a fallen sapling. He inspected – yes, it was a small tree trunk but trimmed, hardened, how many years ago? Could it be as many as fifteen years? He grasped the branch. He poked it down the hole under the boulder, then leaned it back against the smaller rock. Yes, he thought, this was it! It was a lever. So he grasped the top of that staff and pulled it down and yes! The boulder lifted.

Next he had to work out how to keep the boulder lifted so he could hunt for whatever was hidden beneath. Looking around, he saw another rock set back with a notch beneath it and so, working hard, he managed to work the lever so low, lifting the boulder so high, that he could jemmy the end of the lever under that third rock. Releasing his hold on the lever, it stayed where he had put it and the boulder stayed lifted. Exploring beneath, he found a long, heavy cloth package. He pulled it out, looked at his mother, mystified.

'Open it,' she said.

He did, and inside he found a sword, a fine sword. His mother was smiling, in part at his wonder and puzzlement.

'This is your father's sword! He told me, when he left, that if our child was a boy, when you were grown enough, to bring you here and set you this puzzle. It was not, he said, a test of physical strength but a test of your ability to think. If you had not that gift, he said, he did not wish you to know of him because then you would not deserve your birthright.'

'Which is?' said Theseus.

'Theseus, your father is Aegeus, the King of Athens! In Athens they think him childless. He says there is too much scheming, too much intriguing, for a child to be safe. He said also that a child raised as a prince would always struggle to grow straight and strong because there are so many temptations to grow a wicked, not a strong character. You are strong, Theseus, you are honest, you are a true prince among men. All your friends look to you for leadership. So, take this sword, travel to Athens, show it to your father and he will know you!'

2

Theseus had been happy in his new life, the life of a prince, and how could he not be? But, even within that first year he had noticed a change come over the people of Athens. Even though the corn grew tall, the grapes and the olives grew green, the swallows skimmed and the birds sang, he sensed a winter creeping into the hearts of the Athenians. People he asked changed the subject and so, eventually, he cornered his father and demanded to know what was wrong. King Aegeus explained, 'Every year we pay tribute to Minos, the King of Crete. Every year we send eighteen youths and maidens, whose names are drawn by lot.'

'And what becomes of them?' Theseus demanded. Aegeus' answer horrified him. They were shown to the King, thrown into an impenetrable maze and they never came out. Hidden at the heart of that maze, the Labyrinth, lurked a monster, the Minotaur, with the body of a man and the head of a bull. The monster devoured them. Theseus wanted to know, 'Why is it called the Minotaur?'

'Because it is his family,' said Aegeus, 'Minos' wife gave birth to it. Most kings have secrets; for years, you were mine.'

6

Now Theseus stood blinking in the light. His right hand still held a short sword that, even now, steamed with the Minotaur's sticky and stinking blood! His left hand still held the ball of twine, not quite wound back up but he could see his way now. He walked triumphantly to the mouth of the Labyrinth. People screamed when they saw him; he was bruised, grazed, dishevelled, and he was covered in blood. But they screamed the more because they had never seen anyone walk out of the Labyrinth before! Their first fear had been that here was the Minotaur come to terrorise them. But no, Theseus told them, their lives could continue as meaninglessly as before, they were safe. The Minotaur was dead, he had killed it and the tribute must stop. Ariadne wanted to rush to him, but waited. That could wait. The news reached the barracks where all the youths and maidens were kept, the news that now they were saved, and the roar that went up, that roar of joy, was more deafening even than the roars of the Minotaur. Theseus had saved them!

5

The Minotaur, a queen's shame and a king's secret. The Minotaur, its powerful human body fed by human flesh! Its frame topped by the massive head of a bull, bull's fur sprouting down its shoulders, chest, back, stomach, groin. Thick legs supported that head, a thick torso also, strong, sturdy arms with powerful hands that tore open the bodies of young men and women. The Minotaur! A beast of hidden shame fed further on injustice. It was dead.

Phew! So, clearly that's not the best way to tell that story, but it can be done and it's quite a limbering-up exercise. It also shows you how a listener can easily make some pretty sideways moves, some intricate connections. Remember, you don't always have to make it too easy for your listeners.

Now it's your turn. Have a few goes and see what you can do. Hopefully, you will notice more clearly what I imagine you've already begun to notice as you've gone through your improvisations so far, that storytelling is at least as much about how you connect ideas as it is about the ideas themselves.

Applying the Four Types of Plot

So, what are some ways in which we can apply the Four Types of Plot to enrich our storytelling? Let's start with one of the easiest, Flashback. Take a story you have already created, or a story you already know, and, if it's a Quest story, start it at stage 5. To make things easy for yourself, make sure your story has only one central protagonist whose story you are telling (and not, for example, 'The Three Little Pigs'). Whatever other kind of story you may have chosen, try starting at the point of maximum emotional intensity. Just jump right in and, having done so, show us, by flashing back in time, how previous events got your protagonist to be in this fix. Then finish it.

Next, Parallel. Take a story you know and another story that follows the same story structure, for example, two Quests and two Rags to Riches stories. See if you can think of two stories that explore a related theme, but perhaps in different ways. Then start your A story and tell Stage 1 and, before going on to Stage 2, start your B story also at Stage 1. Then, swap between the two as you go forward. Don't, this time, have the stories refer to one another, but simply place them side by side and see for yourself what simple juxtaposition does. If this process creates a gap that your listener has to fill, that's perfect! It means they, in order to close the gap (remember the 'fear of empty spaces'?), will have to come further into the story. Next, staying with Parallel but exploring it differently, start a story at 1. Go right through to 5, then use 5 to open another story at 1. Take it up to 5 and do the same again. Then finish all three stories.

Lastly, let's start exploring how you can Nest stories within stories. Do you remember the story you created when we explored Journey and Return? Great; let's tell it to the point where your character, passively, has been moved into another world. Now, in that other world, present them with a Problem that is *not* how to get home. Let them respond to the Problem and now you've sent them off on a Quest. Inside that Quest you may choose to open another, then close it and return to the former and then, when that Quest has finished, pick up the

Journey and Return structure. A simple Nested Narrative runs as first Story A opens, then Story B opens, closes, then Story A closes. This is how, for example, *The Lion, the Witch and the Wardrobe* works, and so too *Gulliver's Travels* and *The Seven Voyages of Sinbad*.

You can develop this further using, for example, a Rebirth story, only this time we are going to Nest stories inside stories, which are themselves Nested, as in, open Story A, then Story B, then C, then D, then close D, then C, then B, then A. So, for example, let's take as our Story A, the tale of 'Thorn Rose'. Let's tell it to the point where Thorn Rose has fallen asleep. Leave her there, and shift your focus to a young prince wandering the countryside. That's the Who and Where of a new, Nested Story B taken care of. He has heard of a beautiful woman imprisoned in a deep sleep and he wants to rescue her. That's Story B's Problem stage, so now you can start his Journey. Is this making sense so far?

What else might you Nest inside the Prince's story? Might he meet, on his journey to find the enchanted castle, a beautiful woman who is desperately travelling the land, looking for a blinded man? What is her name, and how did she come to have such beautiful hair? Her name is Rapunzel, of course, and now you can jump off the Prince's story and tell her story. This is Story C. On her journey, she might mention that she met a prince who was riding home in great distress. Why? He had just been off to a neighbouring kingdom to meet a young woman who might become his wife but his way was blocked by an immense Lindworm who would not let him pass. He can't think what to do. This is Story D. Rapunzel can encourage him, saying that, when she herself was a captive in a tower waiting for someone to come and rescue her and thinking she could never overcome that monstrous enchantress, a bird told her the story of a young man, a king's son, who, in company with seven other youths and eight maidens, was sent as tribute to be devoured by a monster. This is Story E. *She* can tell all of how Theseus overcame the Minotaur, which proves that monsters can be overcome and, when she concludes, she can tell the Lindworm's brother that she did meet her prince, her true love, but now she can't find him. Ah, the Lindworm's brother might say, but is she quite sure her prince is all that he seems? Because he has heard tell of a young woman, called Lady Margaret, who fell deeply in love with a man who seemed perfect, but ...

You can tell the whole story of 'Mr Fox', Story F, then have the Lindworm's younger brother take his leave of Rapunzel and finish his Story D and, when the Lindworm Prince, now human, is on his way to his new peaceful home, he can meet Rapunzel and tell how the Lindworm story, Story D, ends. Then the Prince, who is on his way to rescue Thorn Rose, can tell Rapunzel that he encountered a blind man who said he was looking for his true love. The Prince can unite Rapunzel with *her* prince, her tears can heal his eyes, ending Story C, and Rapunzel's prince can give Thorn Rose's prince directions, now that he can see, to the castle that holds Thorn Rose, and you can finish the Stories B and A that you started first, last. He kisses Thorn Rose, she wakes up and says, 'Have I missed anything?'

Are you following this? Exhausting, I know, and I know that's an awful lot of princes who need to be distinguished from one another, but isn't it exciting, just how much you can do, and just how far you can travel? You can now easily spread the telling of a story over many occasions.[33] If you make a mistake, don't worry, because your listeners *will* correct you. When you Nest narratives, your listeners will have a sense of taking such a deep and deeply involving journey, and when you bring them home again, they will feel such relief and joy! And there's that Journey and Return structure again.

 Parable

I mentioned earlier that we would look at Parable. I don't include Parable among the Nine Forms of Story because I don't think it can be defined as such. It is more a technique of performance.

Parable is created using a form of parallel plot. A story is told either in its entirety and then explained (as in 'now you've heard the story, here is what you should understand from it') or it is told in part then Commented on, then a bit more, then more Comment. Parable is very popular with political, business and religious leaders because it is essentially about telling the audience how to interpret or what to think in response to a story.

For Parable to work there are certain conditions that need apply. I suggest there is, first of all, a precept, principle or point you wish to establish, such as, for example, the importance, for business of a balance between discipline and freedom; for governments, the need to inspire enterprise while protecting the unenterprising or, for women, the need to stay safe when travelling. Once you have a point to make you need to:

1. **Pattern Fit** - find or create a story that can be used as a metaphor extended over time to stand entirely for something else, the real subject of your talk.
2. **Tell Your Parallel Story** - in entirety or by flitting between the two.
3. **Exploration** - multiple features are identified because they will serve to illustrate that which you are really talking about. The metaphor extends over time.

4. **Pattern Bridge** - a statement that connects the metaphorical to the actual. This can either be a 'reveal' at the end when your audience realises why they've been listening to you talk about hedge trimming when they actually thought they were to hear about the Year Plan, or 'Little Red Riding Hood', when they thought they were to discuss gender in the workplace, 'The Good Samaritan' when they thought this was a meeting about the traveller camp that has set up on the village green.

You may have sensed that I personally am not particularly fond of this technique. I feel it can all too easily become ponderous, didactic, even manipulative. But if you need to use it, just make sure you do it well. I feel the more you leave to the intelligence and imagination of your listener, the more powerful the effect. Better that it happens within them than before them.

Ending Up

So now we are approaching the end of our journey together. I do hope you've enjoyed yourself and that you've really begun to apply the techniques detailed in this book. At the start of this journey, I introduced you to the idea that you can, more easily than you might have thought, spontaneously create gripping stories that will delight your listeners. I promised I would teach you how to use simple structures and that I would teach you to memorise these structures in such a way that you would *never* be at a loss if the coach broke down and you had all of Years 4 and 5 to entertain, or if you were stuck in the queue for the ferry, or the hospital and the tablet is out of power, there aren't any books and in any case your child doesn't want to have to look at anything. How have we got on? Have you been able to help me redeem my promise to you? Are you telling stories, conjured as if from thin air? I hope so.

What else can you do now? If you are a teacher, you've probably already spotted the application of all this to your teaching work and you've probably started introducing some of these games into class. Because you can divide children into groups, one child for each stage of a given Form of Story perhaps, and they can work collaboratively to create stories that they then tell to class. Having 'owned' a new story, how much easier is it to take their emotional investment and use it as fuel to power the harder task of writing it down? I've been running literacy workshops like this in schools and universities in the UK and internationally for two decades and some of the stories created have been so good that I could easily just insert them into my performance repertoire and no one would ever guess that they weren't centuries-old folk tales.

Furthermore, and if you're working with older children, you can apply the Forms of Story to your lesson planning and delivery. Learning outcome as the goal of a Quest, for example? Or a story created to provoke a discussion around key topics? Once you know the Forms of Story, it's down to you and your creativity to apply them as you need to. Traditional storytelling is an idiom, and it's an idiom I love, but storymaking itself is much larger. Our ability to create stories to pass on information, embed learning, provoke insight or just delight is, I believe, a fundamental aspect of our nature as human beings. *Homo sapiens*, yes, and also *Homo narrante*.

If you have care of children and you want games to add to your existing repertoire of Winding/Unwinding, Capital Cities or I Spy, then what about you calling out the next stage of a story structure to the kids in the back seat and each child taking it in turns to take the story on, and then you all get to create and tell the story together? Then watch what happens to your children's schoolwork.

I sincerely hope you've had fun travelling through this book with me. I hope you've surprised yourself by discovering that you really *can* make up and tell wonderful stories. I hope you have had magical moments with your stories and the children in your care. I wish you many, many more.

So how should a story end? How should, for that matter, this book end? Traditionally, there are many good ways to end a story: 'And that is the end of the story'; 'And they all lived happily ever after'; or 'This is where our paths divide and may we meet again at another turn of the road in happiness, in health, and in the finest company'?

But in this particular case, I would prefer to say, 'They reached the end and realised it was not an end but a beginning, and they all told happily ever after'.

Thank you for journeying with me.

Giles ;{~

One Last Thing! The Chain Story

Successful storytelling is about making convincing links between elements in a narrative. You will shortly learn how, in some ways, the quality of the links between elements may be even more important than the quality of the elements themselves. At the very least, if you can make good links then slightly ropey content can be got away with.

So a Chain story is a very important element in early years education as it works so directly on language, visualisation and memory. To this day, you probably remember the refrain and, if not the exact words, the rhythm of 'The House that Jack Built'? And you remember the way that the Chain of things, added to with each iteration, would come accelerating and tumbling to that refrain? I'd like to suggest that you can invent your own with a group of young people and that that is the memory that you built.

About the Author

Giles Abbott has been a professional storyteller since 2000 and a voice teacher since 2005, performing all over the UK and internationally to adult audiences at festivals, arts centres, theatres and concert halls. He visits schools as a storyteller and also runs workshops in storytelling skills and voice development in schools, colleges, universities and at public events.

As a storyteller he has created and toured works for adults to commission, such as 'Deirdre of the Sorrows' for Festival at the Edge, 2007; and 'Caught on the Horns' for the Cost of Art Festival, London, 2008. He has created biographically inspired works, such as 'A O Hume – a Life' for the South London Botanical Institute, 2013 and 'Tongues of Flame', the story of Captain Sir Richard Francis Burton, which was funded by Arts Council England, 2013–15. In 2016 he was commissioned by the Pope's Grotto Preservation Trust to create 'A Search For Perfection' which narrates the life of eighteenth century poet Alexander Pope, which still gets performed at the restored grotto.

In 2018–19, Giles ran Blind Tellers in association with the Royal Society for Blind Children and again with the support of Arts Council England; this project enabled Giles to spend a year working with blind and partially sighted young people, teaching them storytelling skills, voice development and rhetorical composition skills to help them with their confidence, self-esteem and self-expression as well as their employability. This work gave blind teenagers the opportunity to tell their own versions of traditional stories to a spellbound audience of more than 200 patrons, parents and supporters of the charity.

Giles' poetry has appeared in *The Spectator* magazine as well as in small press publications. In 2011 he wrote text for 'Song Celestial', a composition by the Indian virtuoso Baluji Shrivastav, and thereafter Giles toured with the group, singing and reciting in English and Sanskrit. A version of this work was reprised in 2018 for a performance in the Queen Elizabeth Hall on London's South Bank. In 2011–12 he worked with composer Lloyd Coleman, on 'Breaking the Wall', a narrative poem that formed the core of an orchestral work by Coleman commissioned by Disability Arts Cymru as part of the 2012 Cultural Olympiad.

A short film, co-written with and directed by Frederic Casella, was released in 2016. *The King* was selected for numerous festivals and won a number of awards.

Giles took his MA in Voice Studies from the Central School of Speech and Drama in 2006, since when he has taught Voice to acting students at Arts Ed, Birkbeck College, and is currently teaching on many courses at Identity School of Acting, also at MetFilm School and City Lit, all in London. He has taught storytelling workshops at the Academy of Live and Recorded Arts, the Drama Centre, the Central School of Speech and Drama, and for schoolteachers on behalf of the British Council in India in Kolkata, Delhi, Chandigarh, Hyderabad, Bangalore and Mumbai. He has also told stories in numerous schools in Cairo, Egypt, and has performed three years running at the International Shakespeare Festival held at Theatr Globe in Neuss, Germany. He has taught workshops in Storytelling and Communication for undergraduates at the University of Darmstadt and at Heinrich Heine University, both in Germany, and also for students at the University of Exeter and University of Wolverhampton.

As a consultant, Giles has combined his skills in voice and storytelling to teach staff at companies such as Fox International Channels, Otsuka Pharmaceuticals, Red Bull, Mindshare, HSBC, Citibank, ZYen, Commerzbank, BP and many others. His consultancy was used by the Science Museum, London, to create the text to guide thousands of visitors around an entire wing, telling the story of Modern Communication Technology. He has run storytelling and storymaking workshops for thousands of schoolchildren in the UK.

Giles is a voice artist and has recorded numerous voice-overs for *Sunny Bank Allotments*, an animated series for preschool children, also audiobooks, internal communications and advertisements. His voiceover work on the Smouldering Disease campaign won Gold Medal at the PM Society Awards and in 2015, for Valentine's, Giles is the voice of Dr Pepper. He is represented by Soho Voices.

An actor, in 2023 Giles created the role of William Walter, the Tinker, in Olivia Foan's play *The Tinker*, staged as part of Vault Festival. Giles played the role of MC in UCAN Theatre's *The Palais* in 2025 in the Sherman Theatre, Cardiff. All actors were blind and all played sighted characters.

In 2024–25 Giles worked with the Museum of Story in Oxford to create a new kind of 'immersive and narrative' audio description (AD). This was based on groundbreaking research by Hannah Thompson into creating crowd-sourced and engaging AD. Giles attended whilst blind children explored the collection, then, using transcripts and more, created and voiced the new Audio Description of the Museum. The Museum's ambition was 'to create an experience sighted people would want to be part of!'

How did all this start? Giles's first degree was in English Language and Literature, from St Catherine's College, University of Oxford, in 1993. In 1998 Giles suffered sudden and severe sight loss and he is now registered blind, having lost the ability to pick up and read a book in just four hours during a coach journey from Leeds to London. Exiled from literacy, Giles rediscovered something he didn't know he'd lost, the elemental joy of listening to and telling stories. Hopefully, this book has done something to connect or reconnect you to that joy too.

www.gilesabbott.com
info@gilesabbott.com

Author photos © David X Green

Endnotes

1 Yes, reader, I am, as I write this, in my early fifties. Shhh! G ;{D~

2 We were living in Todmorden, in the Calder Valley, West Yorkshire, and the town down the valley was Hebden Bridge. G :{~

3 In a bookshop. A blind man in a bookshop is kind of like a vegan in a butchers? G :{D~

4 This also goes back to my mother, the English teacher. She had worked with a kid I knew in childhood, one of her friend's sons, and had helped get him the diagnosis and support he needed for his dyslexia and I remembered what she had told me about the symptoms. G ;{~

5 Seldom a change, usually just the front of a small room but it felt like the O2 Arena to me! G :{~

6 Alright, maybe Cicero never said this. But don't you wish he had?

7 Birmingham-based storyteller and promoter Graham Langley, who has been a tremendous force in storytelling for most of his adult life, once said this to me as we discussed the work of an early-career storyteller. I have had many reasons to remember this since.

8 Another gem, this time from Nir Paldi of the brilliant physical theatre group Theatre Ad Infinitum.

9 Many people in many disciplines have written and taught about this aspect of story. I personally learned these specific terms from Ben Haggarty of the Crick Crack Club, who has been personally responsible for spearheading and simultaneously defining the revival of traditional storytelling to adults since the 1980s. I can't recommend his work highly enough.

10 Ben Haggarty is, simply put, one of the best storytellers in the world. His pioneering work with Hugh Lupton and Sally Pomme Clayton, working together as the Company of Storytellers, did a huge amount in reviving traditional storytelling for adults in the UK. The Crick Crack Club is still one of the UK's leading promoters and proponents of traditional storytelling, and if you want to know how magical, how raw, real storytelling can feel, I cannot recommend them highly enough.

11 I have to – I can't see my audience.

12 I am English, so one will have to do. This is not a boast, more an admission ...

13 There is a story in the Grimm brothers' collection called 'The Juniper Tree', which is very similar.

14 'Mr Fox', by the way, is a traditional English story Shakespeare knew. In *Much Ado About Nothing*, Benedick says, 'Like the old tale, my lord: "It is not so nor 'twas

not so but, indeed, God forbid it should be so".' I learned the story from Graham Langley in a pub in Whitby sometime in the last ten years, with an almost identical refrain, and yet, to Shakespeare, it was already an old tale! I love the idea that I can spook modern children with a story that probably once spooked the young William Shakespeare.

15 This is a direct quote from legendary Scots traveller-storyteller Duncan Williamson. Duncan told us that one Christmas his father shared with his children one orange, so one peg each. Then he said, 'That was nice, but now it's gone. So I'm going to give a gift now that you'll always have ...'

16 In iambic pentameter if they heard me learning *Macbeth*.

17 You could argue that all dream narratives are a Journey and Return story, even something as corny as Bobby Ewing's miraculous resurrection after dying two series earlier in '80s soap opera phenomenon *Dallas*.

18 Indeed, in medieval European folklore there is a world called the Land of Cockaigne, from the French *pays de cocange*, and from which we get (Cloud) Cuckoo Land. This world, imagined by people for whom poor nutrition was an ever-present factor in their lives, is a world where the clouds rain cheeses, where the fence posts are made of sponge fingers, the streams flow with milk and honey and pigs run through the streets with forks in their backs squealing, 'eat me!'.

19 Humour matures, thankfully.

20 Six parts again - you see! you see! ;-)

21 Tales from the Wharf, held on the last Friday of the month in a pub called the Stubbing Wharf, just out of Hebden Bridge. They still meet there every month. It's where I began learning my trade and if they ever stop meeting there, then as far as I'm concerned, Doomsday is near.

22 Does that experience strike any dim bells? 'He/she's nice! I wish they'd come over and talk to me! Come on! Oh my God, they're coming over. *Paniiiiic!*'. ;-)

23 You will learn more about framing devices when you start to explore Types of Plot (page 187).

24 I don't know why this particular element exists and, from a political point of view, I'll admit I'm uncomfortable with it. Does it mean that we as storytellers have to imply that the only characters who deserve riches are those who were originally rich at birth and who have thus been wrongly impoverished? Certainly, that would have been Charles Perrault's view when he wrote down his version of *Cinderella* in the seventeenth century. But why can't poor people deserve to be enriched? Is it simply that a memory of better times accentuates the misery of deprivation? I honestly don't know.

25 I know, a stock broker, a prostitute? How did they ever manage to get such an implausible scenario through the script development stage?

26 I told a version of *Gilette of Narbonne* by Bocaccio, which is the narrative basis of Shakespeare's *All's Well that Ends Well*.

27 Christopher Brooker, in his *The Seven Basic Plots*, gives 'Perseus and Andromeda' as his example of what he calls 'Overcoming the Monster'. I think this lacks clarity. There's no discovery stage here, so what makes 'Perseus and Andromeda' in any way different from a Quest? Erm, nothing.

28 I learned about this and its application to story from Leon Conrad. Leon is a twenty-first-century polymath (linguist, musician, writer, philosopher) and his book *Story and Structure* is essential if you wish to take this research into structure into more mathematical depth.

29 From Kipling's *Just So Stories* but almost certainly an Indian folk story in origin.

30 Many and various, so in Ancient Greece, a talented weaver, Arachne, boasts that she is a better weaver even than the goddess Athena. Athena challenges her to prove it and, because she does, punishes her by turning her into the spider. While in the Caribbean, the descendants of enslaved Africans took the character of the powerful trickster god Kwaku Anansi and shrunk him down so very small that you might not even notice how strong and clever he was. In fact, better that you don't ...

31 I know this one too well myself. It's years now since I've been able to see well enough to distinguish my toes and, when cutting my toenails in a hurry ... G ;{~

32 As previously stated, much of my repertoire is made up of stories I have never seen in written form.

33 Potentially, even one thousand and one nights? More than one bedtime, at any rate, and just think how this is working to develop not only your own but also your child's powers of recall and concentration, not to mention imagination and empathy.

Since 1993, The Society for Storytelling has championed the ancient art of oral storytelling and its long and honourable history – not just as entertainment, but also in education, health, and inspiring and changing lives. Storytellers, enthusiasts and academics support and are supported by this registered charity to ensure the art is nurtured and developed throughout the UK.

Many activities of the Society are available to all, such as locating storytellers on the Society website, taking part in our annual National Storytelling Week at the start of every February, purchasing our quarterly magazine Storylines, or attending our Annual Gathering – a chance to revel in engaging performances, inspiring workshops, and the company of like-minded people.

You can also become a member of the Society to support the work we do. In return, you receive free access to Storylines, discounted tickets to the Annual Gathering and other storytelling events, the opportunity to join our mentorship scheme for new storytellers, and more. Among our great deals for members is a 30% discount off titles from The History Press.

For more information, including how to join, please visit

www.sfs.org.uk